Aristide Maillol: 1861-1944

This exhibition is supported by grants from *Les Amis de Maillol*, Paris,
and The National Endowment for the Arts in Washington, D.C., a Federal Agency.

The Solomon R. Guggenheim Museum, New York

Published by The Solomon R. Guggenheim Foundation
New York, 1975
ISBN: 0-89207-000-5
Library of Congress Card Catalogue No. 75-42576
© The Solomon R. Guggenheim Foundation, 1975
Printed in the United States

4

PREFACE AND
ACKNOWLEDGEMENTS

THOMAS M. MESSER, DIRECTOR
The Solomon R. Guggenheim Museum

The more than eighty years of Aristide Maillol's life are evenly divided between the nineteenth and twentieth centuries, making him, more than most of his contemporaries, a figure of transition from one era to another. Early in his development he lessened his dependence upon academic traditions in painting and sculpture by emulating Gauguin's primitive and Symbolist art which he deeply admired. Maillol's art subsequently developed in close consonance with Maurice Denis and other Nabis painters. His painting, drawing and tapestry, and to some degree even the sculpture of this period, reflected the Nabis' creative ideals. Through more than four decades of the twentieth century, Maillol proceeded to purify and intensify his early achievements, thereby composing a lifework in which stylistic subdivisions largely disappear within a unity imposed by an intense plastic striving. These artistic goals were realized, to a preponderant degree, in sculptures of the female form captured in attitudes of voluptuous calm and repose. Maillol achieved sculptural monumentality by closely observing his models and by effectively idealizing their forms.

The concept of innovation, so basic to twentieth-century art, is disdained by Maillol who concedes freely that "I do not invent anything, just as the apple tree cannot pretend to have invented its apples." And, for related reasons, unlike Giacometti for instance, he felt no compulsion to come to terms with Cubism or Surrealism but continued to nourish himself through native traditions that seemed to flow into his increasingly earthy and potent sculptural expression.

Far from remaining a primitive as a result of such self-containment, Maillol in his art aspires to and often merges with currents that have, ever since the age of Phidias, determined the timeless flow of Mediterranean sculpture. For the modern beholder, therefore, Maillol's sculpture, painting, drawing and book illustration provide an interesting challenge: to perceive a modernism that is based on *classical* traditions and that exists in contra-distinction to the *archaic* modes of African, and exotic origin that have dominated our era ever since Picasso created the *Demoiselles d'Avignon.*

Individual works by Aristide Maillol have been seen in many public and private collections but no attempt to present them in a retrospective exhibition sequence has ever been made in a New York museum. This institutional neglect is probably due in part to a lack of interest shown in recent decades for Maillol's idealizing art. Another factor was no doubt the monumental dimensions and the great weight of Maillol's sculptures, which in addition to the overwhelming demands they imposed upon museum space, also threatened diminishing exhibition budgets. The current show, therefore, could not have been mounted without the decisive financial aid received from the National Endowment for the Arts in Washington, D.C., and the Friends of Maillol in Paris. Mme. Dina Vierny, as Executrix of Maillol's estate, and Klaus Perls, the artist's principal New York dealer, have made generous contributions through the latter organization.

Maillol's sculptures, paintings and works on paper were diligently sought out and selected by Linda Konheim, Program Administrator, and installed under the supervision of Orrin Riley, Technical Administrator, both staff members of the Guggenheim Museum. Judith Siegel assisted in all preparatory phases of the exhibition. Miss Konheim also compiled the catalogue with the aid of the Museum's Editor, Carol Fuerstein. As is invariably the case in demanding undertakings of this kind, virtually every Museum department has been involved and has contributed its efforts.

The catalogue benefited importantly from John Rewald's introductory essay, based on his personal reminiscences of Aristide Maillol. He and Dina Vierny lent, for the exhibition as well as the catalogue, their expertise and technical knowledge. Both have also contributed important documents from their private files and enriched the publication by allowing us to reproduce photographs in their possession. Together with Klaus Perls and Alexandre Rosenberg they provided invaluable help in locating works.

Many individuals, museums and galleries, listed separately, have generously loaned their prized possessions to aid this rare and important occasion. To these and others whose names must be omitted in order to limit credits to the most conspicuous contributors, we extend our warmest thanks and gratitude.

MAILLOL REMEMBERED

JOHN REWALD

Checklist numbers in parenthesis are either the works discussed or closely related pieces.

This story begins almost fifty years ago when a high school boy from Hamburg went as an exchange student to London. There, in the Tate Gallery, he discovered a work that moved him more deeply than anything he had ever seen. It was a powerful female torso of what seemed to him incredible plastic intensity, a human form that appeared dynamic and yet self-contained, monumental but also sensuous, and of imposing splendor. Its beauty and bursting vitality stirred him profoundly. He returned again and again to this massive, over-life-size piece and, in a small notebook, made little sketches of it, turning slowly around the large bronze, studying the undulations of the belly, the profile of the strutting breasts, the muscles of the thighs, the curve of the spine, the firmness of the back. He "appropriated" every inch of this glorious body.

A plaque on the socle said that this was the torso of *L'Action enchaînée* (52), a monument to Blanqui, that it was by Aristide Maillol, a Frenchman born almost seventy years before, and that the sculpture had been recently acquired.

Upon his return to Hamburg the boy began to look for other works by the artist. He did not find any in the local art museum, but in the nearby museum for applied arts there was, in a hallway, a vitrine with numerous small, lovely terra cottas. Some of these were by a Polish sculptor living in Paris, Moïse Kogan, the others by Maillol. And the enchantment with his work started all over again in front of these exquisite little figures of girls sitting or bending or squatting, standing or lying or kneeling, each a wonder of perfection, of charm and harmony. The same man who had

struck the most vibrant accents of a full orchestra in the big bronze torso had conjured up the most delicate strains of a violin in these tiny and brittle nudes.

At home, the boy tried to fashion—with the help of his sketches and of photographs—a copy in plasteline of the torso, but he soon found out that size is an inalienable part of the artist's concept and that what was overpowering on a large scale could not be duplicated in any other format, just as the beauty of the terra cottas was intimately linked to their smallness.

The student also gathered books about the artist, of which there were a few. Maillol had found early recognition in Germany where Count Kessler had sponsored him, had published the first of his books illustrated with woodcuts, had commissioned a male figure and had taken him on a trip to Greece. There Maillol had found a countryside that closely resembled the foothills of the Pyrenees where he was born. Maillol's young admirer read of his village, Banyuls, on the shores of the Mediterranean (that word alone had a flavor of paradise to a youngster raised on the North Sea), of his studio surrounded by fig trees and vineyards (plants he had never seen), of a tall bearded sculptor, a cross between a fisherman and a peasant, who sometimes worked on the beach and who spoke Catalan (sounds he could not even fathom). It all appeared so deliciously unreal and just as exotic as Gauguin's heaven in Tahiti. It was something to be read and dreamt about yet never to be experienced.

But then the high school pupil became an art-history student (in those days Panofsky was teaching in Hamburg) and went to France

... the large bay of Banyuls suddenly lay before us.

to study Romanesque and Gothic architecture and, of course, sculpture as well. From Naumburg and Bamberg his way led to Reims and Chartres, to Dijon and Moissac· There it stopped. Somehow, somewhere the appeal of more recent works became so strong that, from the Musée de Cluny he turned to the Impressionist collections (then still rather modest) of the Louvre. And as he met people interested in these and in even more modern, actually still living artists, he ran into a critic who spoke casually of Maillol, the way one speaks of an old acquaintance. It was incredibly easy to obtain an introduction and to simply go and call on him.

That day my heart was beating so fast that I do not remember anything that happened, neither what was said nor where it occurred. But it must have been at Marly, outside Paris, where Maillol received visitors every Sunday and where he was always surrounded by a crowd of admirers, friends, dealers, publishers, artists, favor-seekers and celebrity hunters. Maillol, however, noticed the young, awestruck foreigner whose eyes caressed the pieces cluttering the studio. Not many words were exchanged between them amidst all those who were trying to capture the master's attention, but he did tell the timid visitor that he should come to Banyuls during the spring where they would be able to spend a few quiet hours together. With that informal invitation something unbelievable had come true.

In April 1938 I arrived in Perpignan and took the bus to Banyuls. After Port-Vendres and many turns of the road, the large bay of Banyuls suddenly lay before us. The turbulent

I asked for Maillol's house which was pointed out to me, all the way up, among the last ones of the old section, dominating the bay.

Inside, an armless plaster cast of the *Ile de France* detached itself from the penumbra.

sea was gnawing the beach, a strong wind was roughing up the plane trees. The bus slowly descended between houses closely assembled, one behind the other, as though to avoid slipping down the slope and into the water; finally it reached the seaside.

I asked for Maillol's house which was pointed out to me, all the way up, among the last ones of the old section, dominating the bay. Nestled between its neighbors, its only distinction was its pink color. The street rose steeply; in front of every house were a few steps with, on every side, lots of containers of all kinds with flowers. As I pushed the small gate to Maillol's garden, I suddenly found myself surrounded by vegetation. A large pine tree that had lost one of its big branches rose in the center of the tiny plot; in its shade grew cacti of all forms, grass protuded from the stone walls, and everywhere plants in pots and pans, even tin cans. In a corner a plump maid was washing. She led me toward a kind of cellar door, where a tremendous white geranium tried to reach the vault above it, and showed me the large window of the artist's studio, surrounded by ivy. At the entrance a young orange tree filtered the rays of the sun through its leaves and transformed them into luminous spots dancing on the ground. Inside, an armless plaster cast of the *Ile de France* (83) detached itself from the penumbra.

Maillol was standing in front of his easel. He put down his palette and cordially shook my hand, apparently not minding the interruption. Then he showed me the painting on which he was working. It was a large canvas of a female nude, seen almost frontally; one corner of the picture was covered with a piece of newspaper

9

held in place by thumbtacks. He began to talk about the difficulties of working without a model but also insisted on the advantages of this method which demands more reflection and concentration. Yet he felt that progress would be easier if, from time to time, he could see a model and, having done so, proceed from memory.

"I know very well," he said, "that I am ruining this painting by overdoing things and by always going over it some more, but you must understand that I am learning in the process. Besides, there are spots that are coming along nicely and that are holding up well." Then he added that he was very tempted to do nothing but paint and—should he manage to express himself satisfactorily—to give up sculpture altogether.

"You really want to abandon it?" I asked incredulously, and he said yes, because of the many physical difficulties he was experiencing, that the work wore him out on account of his age, and also due to the difficulty of finding somebody who could work under his supervision and spare him the effort of shaping out the large stones.

We sat down on a narrow sofa. Next to it a small table was littered with papers. I recognized the letter I had sent him to announce my arrival; its back was covered with drawings of plants and goats. There was also a terra cotta bust covered with some fabric which the artist planned to represent in a painting. Around the bust were pencils, tools, a small plaster cast; not an inch was left vacant. Through the big window fell a soft light, sifted by the garden's vegetation that almost seemed to invade the studio. Inside the window were

flowers in vases, also more tools and piles of all kinds of objects that looked as though they had been picked up in a garage. Yet all the things, the purpose of which may have escaped the uninitiated, were there to be useful when a plaster cast had to be repaired, a sculpture scraped, a wood block scratched out, an easel mended.

The plaster of the *Ile de France* stood near the tiny stove by the coal scuttle. The sofa and the small table were practically the only pieces of furniture in the not very large room; there were also one or two chairs, folders with drawings and canvases turned against the wall: that was all. Here and there some small statues and, abandoned in a corner, clay sketches that were more or less broken. On the sofa several periodicals with photographs of nudes. Above the small table a reproduction after Leonardo in an old Spanish frame and an original Tahitian monotype by Gauguin.

The conversation turned to Gauguin. "He was as gentle as a lamb, speaking very little," said Maillol. "He was, if you wish, haughty and proud since he suffered when his talent was not recognized, his art not accepted. For me," he continued, "that art was a revelation. The *Ecole des Beaux-Arts*, instead of guiding me, had veiled my eyes. But when I saw Gauguin's paintings from Brittany, I felt that I could work in the same spirit. You understand, I immediately told myself that what I was doing would be all right once Gauguin approved of it. And indeed, twice he admired my tapestries: once at the Paris *Salon* and the following year, 1894, at the exhibition of *La Libre esthétique* in Brussels. At the Paris show they were very well hung, since I myself had picked the place. When, upon leaving, I met him in

Through the big window fell a soft light, sifted by the garden's vegetation that almost seemed to invade the studio.

. . . the *Méditerranée* in the beautiful courtyard of the Perpignan town hall.

the street, he said that he had looked for me everywhere, that I had created the most beautiful object of the *Salon*, and he invited me for a drink."

That happened in 1893, when Maillol, having left the studio of Cabanel, began to weave tapestries until deteriorating eyesight forced him to abandon the loom and take up sculpture instead. The days of weaving, he liked to say, were the happiest of his life. It was then, in 1895, that one of the young girls from Banyuls who helped him with his tapestries became his wife. Gauguin was not exactly enchanted with the news and wrote from Tahiti to a mutual friend: "What annoyances one fatally creates for oneself with that stupid institution, marriage! I see where Maillol is into it: I wish him luck. But I am worried for him and it would really be too bad, for he is a good soul and an artist."

From Gauguin the conversation shifted to Vollard, that peculiar figure whose name Maillol always pronounced *Voleur* (thief). He told me how Vollard, in the early days, would buy his small terra cottas to have them cast in bronze. The artist would specify that the editions should be limited to ten casts; he added with resignation: "Well, he made ten casts, all right, except they turned out to be ten thousand!"

As dusk began to invade the studio we walked up the stairs leading to a terrace and to the living room, the largest room of the house. While dinner was being prepared, we sat near the fireplace where a few logs were burning, for the evenings were still chilly. Near the fireplace stood a large wireless and phonograph; Maillol liked to listen especially to Mozart after the day's work was done. He played for me a record of Catalan songs and

dances of a quaint and captivating sonority. Through the windows the bay of Banyuls slowly sank into the night.

We talked about his works in the region: the war monuments of Banyuls, Céret, Port-Vendres and Elne, as well as the *Méditerranée* (46) in the beautiful courtyard of the Perpignan town hall. On the mantlepiece was a small terra cotta of infinite grace, a young girl seemingly carried away by the winds, abandoning her lithe body to the breeze, a drapery unfolding behind her. It was *L'Air* (107), a study of about 1900 which the artist had dug out from among old sketches because he had been approached to do a memorial for French aviation pioneers, particularly Jean Mermoz, to be erected in Toulouse. His project having been approved, he was now faced with the problem of deriving from this piece of only a few inches an over life-size sculpture.

We passed into the small dining room with blue walls, on one of which hung a large portrait of the artist's aunt, the very one who had raised him in this house. She is seen in profile, seated, thin and tall; her expression has the authority and tenderness of an old spinster. This is one of Maillol's early works, when he had not yet discovered sculpture and was still influenced by Puvis de Chavannes, Gauguin and Maurice Denis. Before this painting he spoke again of his beginnings, of the numerous artists misled by poor teaching, to whose number he once had belonged. He considered himself lucky to have escaped, whereas many others, though gifted, "never get anywhere" because they couldn't liberate themselves from the *Ecole des Beaux-Arts*.

At dinner, Maillol ate nothing; he only had a bowl of milk, as he did every evening. He spoke of his favorite authors, especially Plato. "You understand," he said, "for Plato idea and form were one, and that is also how I see it. Form and preconceived idea guide the artist. Force, grace and all the other elements are added in the course of creation and make the product not merely the materialization of an idea, of an intellectual concept, but a work of art."

The meal was served by the plump young maid I had met in the garden. She wore a black dress covered with grease spots; underneath she wore nothing. Whenever she presented a dish and had to lean slightly forward, a generous portion of her natural assets was revealed. Maillol lost nothing of the spectacle, though his eyes did not confine themselves to the decolleté; they followed the girl around, appreciating as well her sturdy bare arms and the movements of her portly hips.

When I returned the next morning, Madame Maillol opened the door for me. She was in a foul mood and made no bones about it. "I can't stand it anymore!" she exclaimed. "I have to do everything myself! Impossible to find decent help in this godforsaken place. I must cook, wash the dishes, do the shopping and clean the house. And all this for. . . ." (Here followed a few heartfelt appreciations of her husband.) I told her how much I sympathized with her and hurried down the stairs to the comparative safety of the studio, where the artist was cleaning his brushes.

Having heard his wife's angry voice, he shook his head. "Sorry, you had to get mixed up in this," he said. "It must be tough on her to be without servants," I replied. "Don't you believe it," he shot back. "She only has herself to blame. Elderly women around here won't work for her because of her nasty disposition. As for the young ones, well, the minute I so much as look at them, they are fired. That's what happened to the girl who served dinner last night."

Maillol then showed me the proofs of his woodcuts for *Daphnis et Chloé (168)*, of which the French edition was being prepared. These woodcuts extend and increase the emotions conveyed by the text. Indeed, the artist had observed, on the spot, the simple events of that tale, where a boy and girl, the earth and the sky, the sea and the mountains were hugging each other. His models were taken from his surroundings: they were the goats of Banyuls, the daughters of wine growers and the sons of fishermen. He seemed to have been inspired by an intimate joy when he traced their pure, tender and touching lines.

Maillol liked to speak of the wood-engravers of the fifteenth century, who combined an exquisite sensibility with often naive simplifications and even awkwardness. It was their spirit that guided him in his woodcuts which — next to his sculptures, drawings and paintings — formed an important aspect of his incessant activity. He did not try to use the wood for effects that imitate drawings or model forms, but endeavored to sum up shapes and gestures in a few lines, while simultaneously trying to create balanced and decorative compositions. Thus he achieved the miracle of preserving the author's quaint poetry without appearing either harsh or sweet, and this in spite of his extreme economy of means. The spare tracings with which he recreated the subjects had a life of their own, an innate grace; they were ingenious and supple and of a touching chastity even when they showed the most intimate embraces of two adolescents discovering love.

"There is everything in that tale Maillol said, "there is a whole world." And he explained that his woodcuts were not to be considered as illustrations in the customary sense, but as images that are part of the text and express the feelings conjured up by the author, as though author and illustrator had conceived the work together. For a long while he spoke of the quality of the paper, of the typography, etc., whose role it is to underline the unity of the prose and its adornments.

Near the window was a large parcel freshly arrived from Paris with wood blocks prepared for illustrations of Virgil's *Géorgiques*. Maillol expressed his admiration for the poet and showed me several small sketchbooks filled with more or less finished studies, ready to be

His shoulders did not seem to feel the weight of his seventy-six years.

cut. They were mostly of trees, all the trees of the region, and all the plants, from the cypress to the acanthus to the humblest: the vine and even the fig tree which Virgil forgot to mention. Sometimes these drawings presented complete compositions or an entire tree, sometimes only a branch, some leaves and a fruit. There were numerous studies of goats, an animal the artist loved above all and whose character he was happy to have grasped. There were still other studies of men and women working in the fields, hoeing, picking fruit, gathering herbs. Some of the drawings were pushed to a high degree of finish, worked and reworked, in others the object observed seemed to have been caught at the first try. All these sketches were done from nature.

It was beautiful outside and we decided to walk to the monument for the war dead with which Maillol had presented Banyuls. He threw a greenish coat, washed out by the rain, over his shoulders; an old Basque beret accentuated his already prominent nose. He walked very straight, without hesitation and without a walking stick. His shoulders did not seem to feel the weight of his seventy-six years. Only his tired eyes appeared to betray a long and not always easy life. His white, not very full beard hid the lines of his mouth.

We went down to the beach. Maillol spoke of his only son, of women, of his love for children and animals. Every now and then we stopped to admire the landscape or glance at the sky, still covered with light clouds. As we passed some pretty girls to whose carriage he drew my attention, the artist began talking again of his trouble with models; he pointed out one of them with whom he would have

The Banyuls war monument stands on a rock in the bay. . . .

liked to work. Yet none of the young local girls would ever dare come to his studio since everybody would know that she had been posing. Only some domestic help might conceivably agree to pose for him if his wife. . . .

How lucky Renoir had been with Gabrielle, who looked after his children, cared for the painter and became an *Odalisque* or a *Bather* when she was not busy with a broom! Maillol remarked that the female type of his preference was exactly the same as Renoir's and that it was also the type of the local women. That made it so difficult for him to find the right kind in Paris, though models were plentiful there. What he was looking for was strong hips, straight legs, heavy arms and a rather full body. (He did not say then that for the last couple of years he had found such a girl, who was posing for him in Marly, Dina Vierny.)

The Banyuls war monument stands on a rock in the bay, attached to the shore by a kind of dike. The project was conceived especially for this site and it was necessary to select a particularly hard stone that would be able to resist the sea. "The harder the stone," the artist explained, "the more pleasant the work, because one can hit more vigorously." We admired the beautiful landscape, the large bay with its calm water, the vineyards descending the slopes and, in the distance, the mountains. The sun had appeared; only a few clouds were left.

We came back for lunch, during which the conversation touched on many subjects. A favorite phrase of Maillol's turned up again and again: "People are stupid and imbeciles." He repeated it on every possible occasion: regarding bad photographs of sculptures, books that

were poorly bound, ugly houses or monuments put in the wrong spot . . . whenever he was displeased with something. His favorite century was that of Louis XIV when artists were respected instead of being treated with contempt; in that happy period, he said, even artisans knew how to create artistically, with a feeling for their materials and with infallible good taste.

During the afternoon we took a walk to the large studio that Maillol had had built just outside of Banyuls and where he made use of the space needed for the execution of large pieces. He didn't work there at that time but planned to use it again for *L'Air*.

On the way we discussed the difficult question of the extent to which the public at large understands art. Maillol was convinced that it didn't and once more expressed his disdain for most people. "I hate them," he repeated, "they are wretched beings. I prefer my cat or a frog. My cat at least understands when I talk to him." As he said this, he drew my attention to the white-tailed blue swallows flying low over the road ahead of us. He showed me trees, stopped to look at flowers, spoke of the vine-stocks, of fertilizers and of the advantage of manure, of droughts and rains; all this in the most natural tone, like a man who has always been close to the soil.

Every now and then, on the road, gendarmes —single or in clusters—controlled the traffic toward the nearby border. Sometimes, Maillol said, he could see, in the evening, fires beyond the mountain range. Yet here around us reigned perfect peace and it was difficult to imagine that barely eight miles away a murderous civil war was raging in Spain.

We approached the studio. Near the small path leading from the road to the building, several blocks of marble—dumped helter-skelter —were awaiting the artist's chisel. As we climbed that path, we discovered everywhere brutally cut bushes, uprooted cacti, broken branches, flowers that had been trampled . . . victims of a savage vandalism. Maillol stood there, surrounded by a serene landscape, by vineyards, olive groves and rocks; sad and numbed he bent down tenderly toward all the mutilated plants, in touching grief.

The large studio was almost empty. One could see that the artist had not used it for some time. In front of a plaster cast of the monument at Céret he explained how he regretted not to have followed his first project for this work which he now preferred to the final version. Having locked doors and shut-

During the afternoon we took a walk to the large studio that Maillol had had built just outside of Banyuls. . . .

ters, we returned to the road and crossed over to the ancient hamlet of Banyuls, somewhat inland from the small port. In Catalan, Maillol chatted with the peasants, admired a donkey, inspected some freshly caught fish, teased a child, talked to a skinny dog that was following us. A peasant himself, tall, straight, walking without fatigue in his worn espadrilles, in good spirits because the sun had come out, he was happy when people greeted him, when they spoke to him in the picturesque language of his native province, for he passionately loved this earth, the men and women whom he had watched grow up, the houses that had not changed since is distant childhood. "You must admit," he proudly said to me, "that this is the most beautiful corner of France. It is an admirable country and I know of nothing like it."

He led me through small, very clean and well-kept gardens, with vegetables and flowers, with lemon trees and rosebushes heavy with blossoms. We walked between two rows of pomegranate trees, their tender green foliage livened by new leaves of a luminous red. "It's divine!" the artist exclaimed repeatedly. But he also expressed great concern at seeing these living hedges replaced by sad wire fences.

A child came out of a house, ran toward Maillol, greeted him cheerfully and walked along with us, a bottle for oil under her arm. Without any timidity she informed the smiling old man that she would soon be eight and that this was the first time she wore her white sandals. Then we shook hands, she curtsied slightly and disappeared into one of the shops near the port.

As we reached the beach, I too took leave while Maillol continued to walk up the steep street to his house where he planned to open the package with wood blocks and transcribe on them his drawings for Virgil's *Géorgiques*.

Maillol was not alone when I came to his studio the next morning. With him were two of his old friends, a physician and a professor, who together admired proofs of the *Daphnis et Chloé* illustrations. Later all four of us went down to the beach where the wind had risen again. Maillol spoke and we listened. "We are the inheritors of the eighteenth century," he explained, "and I have been told that Rodin said exactly the same thing. Yet Rodin copied nature too closely. Where he is strong, as in his *St. Jean-Baptiste*, he is so almost in spite of himself. His male figures generally are not real men because his observation of the model is not sufficiently tempered by a preconceived idea."

The tempestuous genius of Rodin had dominated the period in which Maillol turned to sculpture. In painting, Puvis de Chavannes and, later, Gauguin had already promulgated a certain archaism, but Maillol's first naive statuettes carved directly in wood, and the clay figures he soon modeled, seemed in completed opposition to the prevailing trends: to the emotional style of Rodin, extended further by Bourdelle. What Maillol wanted was neither more nor less than to bring sculpture down to earth again, to make it conscious once more of its weight and of classic stability, rather than to pursue the fascinating union of light and shape, movement and illusion that had given birth to so many of Rodin's masterpieces.

"What I am after," he explained, "is architecture and volume. Sculpture is architecture, is equilibrium of masses. This architectural aspect is hard to achieve. I endeavor to obtain it as did Polycletus. My point of departure always is a geometric figure—square, lozenge, triangle—because those are the shapes which stand up best in space."

Then he spoke some more of his difficult beginnings and of the time he did Renoir's bust. The old painter had sat for him for seven days without touching his brushes, so as to better keep the pose. But during the last session the bust collapsed and Renoir seemed even more distraught by the mishap than was Maillol himself. Seeing him with tears in his eyes, gazing at the heap of soft clay that had slipped to the ground, Maillol picked up what was left of the bust and fixed it in a single sitting.

When I left Maillol after that promenade, it was agreed that I should visit him in Marly during the summer.

Marly-le-Roy, summer 1938

In Marly, Maillol occupied a small bourgeois villa in the midst of a garden and trees; he had bought the plot around 1900 (as soon as he began to enjoy modest sales) and had the house built to his instruction. It was a quiet retreat near the famous Marly forest, fairly close to the railroad, yet far enough from Paris to assure calm while at the same time only a short distance from the city with its museums, concerts, exhibitions, etc. By the late thirties, however, Maillol only rarely went to Paris, preferring to receive his friends in the studio which was separated from the house by a narrow pathway lined with shrubs.

The studio was surrounded by another small garden bordered by a wooden palisade. Against the large structure stood several sheds where the artist stored the plaster casts or molds for his work. On one side, in a very dark corner, one could distinguish compact masses of molds, held together by ropes, their shapes not always revealing the form of the sculpture whose empty shell they enclosed. On the other side some plaster casts of large pieces were assembled. There were also piles of odd fragments from which protruded here a small arm, there a large finger of a figure that must have been over life-size, elsewhere a head or a portion of a drapery. A series of more or less broken busts covered with spider webs was arrayed on a shelf. At the far end, behind the studio and close to the road, a plaster of the *Monument à Cézanne* (70, 71) stood protected by an extension of the roof; not far from it the gigantic nude of *L'Action enchaînée* was held up by a primitive scaffolding. Among the heteroclite objects two long and slender legs supported the slim and gracious body of a young girl with small breasts and undulating hips. This was a study for the statue of *La France* (100), to be about nine feet high, commissioned for the interior court of the Louvre. Elsewhere, under a tree, a plaster of *La Montagne* (98) detached its lively silhouette from the thick foliage that scarcely let any sun rays filter through. Raindrops, however, had reached it and left their traces on the whiteness of the body.

The ground of the garden was covered with leaves, ivy and grass. Near the door of the wooden fence stood a bronze of a nude woman, *La Seine*, holding to her shoulder a drapery

Among the heteroclite objects two long and slender legs supported the slim and gracious body of a young girl. . . .

Near the door of the wooden fence stood a bronze of a nude woman, *La Seine*. . . .

that cascaded down her side. Next to the entrance of the studio, a crouching woman had been put on a crate, her pensive attitude honoring the memory of Claude Debussy. In this setting of foliage and greens her pale form seemed almost surreal, an apparition of a dream listening to the murmur of the winds.

Maillol was working in his studio with a young sculptor, brother of the painter van Dongen, who helped prepare his stones. He himself was putting the finishing touches on two of his *Trois Nymphes* (97) before they were cast to rejoin a third, single (and central) figure already acquired by the Tate Gallery in London. He was busy with the finger of one of the two nudes, having put the detached hand on the marble back of a crouching woman near the large bay window. He was seated, but the hand that he retouched was placed almost at the height of his head, which made working rather uncomfortable. While proceeding with his task, he spoke of the pewter statues at Versailles, of their natural grace and of the apparent ease with which they seem to have been executed. He also marvelled at the elegance and harmony with which they were integrated into the grandiose design of the park. Once, he told me, when he was forty, it had been his dream to animate such a natural setting with sculptures. "Let them give me a garden," he had written to a friend, "a large garden, and I shall people it immediately with statues that will sing . . . among the flowers, for I am also a gardener, you know." But he had never had an opportunity to carry out that dream.

Talking and working, Maillol got up to contemplate a small plaster cast of a naked young girl to whose thighs a piece of cloth had been nailed, indicating the drapes that would cover her modesty; between the folds a long and slender leg emerged like a column. This was another study for *La France*. With one of his tools he scraped the belly of the figure and with his fingers followed her slim form. Then, turning to his apprentice, he gave him directions about how to attach the arm of one of the Nymphes. Finally, he went back to the hand, now working on it standing up but soon complaining that the effort was too tiring for him. Before he sat down again, he once more supervised the work of his assistant while roaming among his statues, caressing one, turning another around, slightly retouching a third.

Seated, Maillol returned with an angry voice to one of his constant gripes: people who do not know anything about art, who have no sense of beauty, who only come to his studio driven by snobbishness or curiosity. Timidly I tried to explain that their ignorance and lack of sensitivity were partly the result of an incomplete and even faulty education. He willingly admitted that this was one of the origins of the problem, but when I tried to expand on the question he got carried away. "Won't you shut up!" he said vividly, yet without meanness and in a tone of mock menace. Then he smiled warmly at me and changed the subject.

Maillol's studio at Marly was much larger, higher and better lit than the one looking out on his garden at Banyuls. In spite of the many plaster casts that crowded it, there was ample room for work and a discreet visitor could even walk around and study the many sculptures while the artist continued with his task, every now and then breaking the silence with a few words.

In spite of the many plaster casts that crowded [the
studio] there was ample room for work. . . .

On a sill running below the window innumerable
small plaster casts and terra cottas were arrayed without any order. . . .

Immediately at the right of the entrance stood the powerful figure of *Pomone* (63), a splendid nude of large and round forms, a symbol of nature and health, but also of the female type that the artist preferred to all others. Next to her was a big couch where models occasionally posed, and nearby a small iron stove whose pipe rose incongruously to the ceiling surrounded by a row of plasters. Among these were the third of the *Trois Nymphes*, *La Vénus au collier* (72), *L'Ile de France*, and yet another *Pomone* (105), this one with her arms hanging down. On a shelf were assembled small clay sketches, most of them broken. Large folders with drawings were leaning against the wall, and there was also one of Maillol's early tapestries in subdued colors, as though faded.

In one corner stood a big male torso near a great wooden door that led to the shed where the *Monument à Cézanne*, *L'Action enchaînée* and other large pieces were stored. All along the wall opposite the entrance was an immense bay window beyond which one perceived trees and *La Montagne*. On a sill running below the window innumerable small plaster casts and terra cottas were arrayed without any order, their outlines detaching themselves darkly against the light falling through the window.

A small table covered with papers and drawings stood in a corner near the marble of the crouching woman on whose back Maillol had placed the hand with which he was busying himself. Against the other wall were more large and small statues, a torso of a woman held together by strings, several studies of the standing young girl with a drapery wrapped around her hips, preparations for the large version of *La France* that was waiting in a shed outside until Maillol would have finished *L'Air* and could begin work on this project.

Next to a barrel stood a model for a monument in the Basel cemetery, half hidden by an easel with a canvas begun in Banyuls. A plaster cast of *La Méditerranée* (46) was set against a wall covered with drawings. There were drawings also on the couch, as well as photographs of nudes; others were lying around all over the place. The drawings dated from many different periods, some of them twenty years old, if not more. Maillol explained that he wouldn't part with any of these, "not even for a million," because he used them constantly for his work and that he actually regretted many of those that he had sold long ago. "You understand," he said, "in those days I thought I could always do others, but there isn't time enough and one doesn't always find the right model." Indeed, for him drawings—and especially drawings from life—were an essential element for his work as a sculptor. According to him it was possible to make a statue after a good drawing; in order to prepare *La France,* he went through his old studies to assemble sketches that he could use for this figure. And while he thus spoke, he took one of his drawings and held it close to the plaster with the drapery around the hips to compare lines and forms.

On one occasion, Maillol told me to select for myself a drawing from one of the heaps on the couch. I picked a very early one, figuring that it would no longer be of use to him, but with an embarrassed smile he said that he might still need it. My second choice was no more successful. Finally, Maillol himself chose a drawing for me and actually gave me *two* to make up for his apparent lack of generosity.

Maillol's drawings were quite unequal in quality, but he was not really interested in their degree of artistry so much as he was in a movement, a specific observation, a detail and—probably—also the recollection of a body conjured up by a few often hasty lines or by a very finished study reproducing the forms of a maid, a woman or a young girl who had once posed for him· Thus many a sketch that may appear to be of scant interest is so important to him that he cannot do without it.

One can generally distinguish two different types among Maillol's drawings: those that were done from a model and that—independent from their greater or lesser "finish"—show his desire to stay close to the elements provided by nature; and those done from memory. These are almost always inspired by some decorative preoccupation: simplified lines are harmoniously assembled and convey a more general aspect in order to achieve compositions in which the body is, so to speak, a pretext for arabesques of great beauty.

"I do not invent anything," Maillol used to say, "just as the apple tree cannot pretend to have invented its apples." Thus, from the form *observed* the artist proceeded to a design where observation and imagination are happily combined. His many tiny notebooks were filled with sketches made on the spot but the movement of a girl seen in the street was eventually "purified" to become a study of her nude body. Yet for his sculptural work he preferred drawings that had remained as close as possible to the model. In this way a sculpture often became the result of a preconceived idea, executed with the help of studies done from nature. "What I want," Maillol explained, "is that the young girl depicted in a statue should represent all young girls, that the woman and her promise of maternity should represent all mothers."

As the afternoon light dimmed, Maillol ceased work and went to fetch a copy of the new French edition of *Daphnis et Chloé* which he displayed with unconcealed pride. I had the impression that this was his favorite among the many books he had illustrated. He now had begun to tackle the woodcuts for Virgil's *Géorgiques*, for which I had seen sketches at Banyuls and of which he showed me some of the first proofs.

On my next visit to Marly we discussed a book I wished to write about him. Maillol took me around in the small garden, indicating the angle from which he wished me to photograph the monument to Debussy. He spoke at length about the importance of the proper height for a socle of a sculpture and of his distaste for photographers who adopted "original" viewpoints: from above, below, at a stilted angle, etc. He felt that photographs should stress the aspects on which the artist himself had insisted; in his case frequently frontal or back view, or profiles. And he preferred an even light to dramatic interpretations. He also disliked photographs in which the background became too important or dwarfed the sculpture, as well as those where the piece detached itself too harshly from a black and dull backdrop; he wanted photographs to be cropped closely around the softly lit work.

I was to follow these guidelines for my forthcoming book, for which I submitted every single illustration to him. He rejected a few of these and instructed me as to how certain pieces should be shown.

The problem of dating his works was more difficult because Maillol himself was totally indifferent to dates and in most cases could not remember when he had executed them. As we went over the photographs for the illustrations and I constantly asked "When?," he often shrugged his shoulders until he finally hit upon a reference concerning his only child. "Lucien was two when I did this," he would say, or "This was done the year Lucien first went to school," or "This dates from the time Lucien was in the army." I carefully scribbled on the back of every photograph: *Lucien age two, Lucien in school, Lucien in army*, etc. After our work was done and all pictures had been annotated, I rushed to see Madame Maillol in the kitchen and asked: "Would you kindly tell me when Lucien was born?" The only trouble with this system was that it turned out to be highly unreliable. Indeed, research has since established that many works had been shown at the *Salon d'Automne* or elsewhere before Lucien had reached the age indicated by his father (Maillol also was one year off for the date of Renoir's bust).

Clotilde Maillol, a plump old woman, bitter and without any grace, once had played an important role in her husband's work. "I lifted her chemise and I found marble," he used to say admiringly of their early years, but those days were long since gone. Now she looked with a sour face at many of the photographs I showed her. Although at the beginning the

majority of her husband's works had represented her, she had been slowly dislodged from his creative activity. *La Nuit* (43), *La Méditerranée*, *L'Action enchaînée* had been posed for by her, and so had innumerable drawings that he still used. Probably more acutely than most married women, she had helplessly watched her man lose interest in her and, what is worse, had also been *replaced* in his work. The many pieces not representing her did not —as far as she was concerned—carry the titles under which they had become famous (titles often provided by Maillol's literary friends): *Ile de France, Flore, Pomone, Les Trois Nymphes*, but were merely the bodies of rivals, and she would spit out designations such as *"une Parisienne," "une gamine de Banyuls," "une voisine de Marly," "Marie,"* etc. A tragic victim of her advancing age, she had lost her husband in more than one way. It was true that Maillol did not help when he once tried to appease her by saying: "But you can still pose for me . . . from the back!" She never forgave him for that.

So they lived side by side without communicating; she cantankerous, he withdrawn into his work, silent and avoiding to provoke her bad temper. Yet her disposition needed no provocation to get the better of her and fill the household with the insufferable tension created by an aggrieved and unreconciled woman. Nor did she make any attempt to conceal her rancor; it was there, in the open, and even the innocent visitor felt himself drawn into the conflict between the two whose exuberant love-making had been witnessed long ago by all the hills around Banyuls, as Maillol sometimes said. Thus the visitor became a witness for whose sympathy vied both an aggressive, neglected and sadly wronged woman and a venerable old man who tried to escape from the oppressive atmosphere of his home, seeking refuge in his studio and in his work.

Once, while we were busy with the book at Marly and lunchtime approached, Maillol stepped out of the studio and shouted across the garden: "Clotilde, would you have a third cutlet?" The shrill answer from the house was short and to the point: "No!"

Banyuls, March 1941

Despite the passage of almost forty years, memories of the last war are still excruciatingly painful. Maillol, close to eighty, now witnessed his third war. He had been ten when the Second Empire crumbled before the Prussian attack; during the First World War he had known the anguish of a father whose only son was serving in the air force. Presently he saw the lamentable agony and demise of the Third Republic. Although in no way involved in politics, he suffered acutely from the situation, one of the consequences of which was that he could not set foot in the occupied zone to finish the several works in progress left behind at Marly. Among these was a large statue of a woman stabbed, prostrate and violently struggling, commissioned in memory of Henri Barbusse as an allegory on the extermination of all wars. (While Maillol himself was not exactly a liberal, the monuments he did or had wished to do were all connected with fighters for great liberal causes: Blanqui, a socialist and revolutionary who spent the greater part of his life in prison; Zola, the commission for whose monument the artist was heartbroken not to obtain;

and finally Barbusse, a work for which the necessary funds were subsequently stopped.) Unfinished, too, in Marly, was the tall figure of *La France*.

But at least Maillol was safe in Banyuls where he could work and where he became increasingly absorbed in painting. Severe restrictions began to make life very difficult, especially since the crops were poor and since the fishermen used their catches for barter rather than selling them; yet even during the most trying periods Dina, who had come to Banyuls to pose for Maillol, always managed to hunt up some food. And for distraction there was Wanda Landowska, who was staying in the village before proceeding to New York. Maillol, who had a passion for music, loved listening to her while she practiced on the harpsichord. He occasionally drew her agile fingers flying over the keyboard.

After internment and a harrowing flight from Paris, a city wide open to Hitler's onrush, I had headed in May 1940 for Banyuls where armed police, at the tiny railroad station, asked for my destination. "Aristide Maillol," I told them and climbed up to his house where I decided to wait for him, once his wife's sister had let me in and informed me that he was out. But within half an hour the police knocked at the door, announcing that all frontier regions had just been forbidden to aliens. So I left without even seeing the artist and finally landed in Aix-en-Provence, there biding my time until I had an opportunity to go to the United States. Before leaving, however, I went to pay a last visit to Maillol, secretly admitting to myself that it was by no means sure whether I would ever see him again.

Thus moving around her own axis, his creation seemed
to come to life.

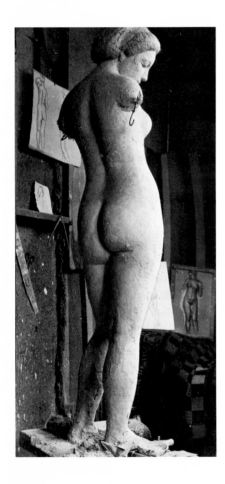 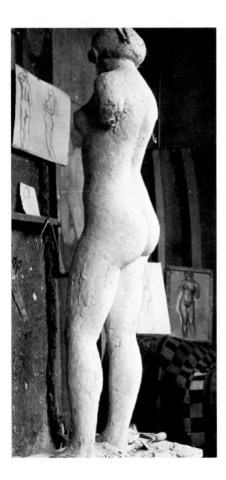 

It was a lovely spring day and a meal—under the circumstances quite sumptuous—was waiting. Yet I was anxious to accompany my host downstairs to his small studio where he had been laboring for several months on a figure of a young girl. As I entered and remained speechless before a life-size plaster without arms, there was in Maillol's eyes a flicker of triumphant joy, and he said in a half ironic, half serious tone:

"You see, I am not too senile yet."

"Oh, you'll never be!" I retorted immediately. But standing next to the sculpture, he sighed:

"What an effort! Four times already she has collapsed, and I find it incredibly difficult to finish the right leg, the bust, and the head, but above all the leg."

(While the artist frequently used clay for small pieces, of which he did fewer and fewer as time passed, he also liked to work directly in plaster, yet he always was rather negligent in establishing the underlying armature so that he often experienced accidents. Another type of mishap had occurred in his early days when he baked his terra cottas, and some of them cracked or crumbled in the oven he had built.)

Maillol now slowly turned the figure on its revolving socle so that I could admire it from all angles. Thus moving around her own axis, his creation seemed to come to life. Slender and almost frail, the young girl appeared even slimmer due to the absence of her arms. Two long legs supported a lithe body with barely blossoming breasts; the head—with eyes half closed—was inclined slightly toward the right shoulder. Once the arms were added, the right hand was to be molded around the breast and

through the lattice-work of the fingers the nipple was to appear. In the hollow of her palm the naked girl would thus be offering a fruit of delight and voluptuousness.

"She will be something like the symbol of a rose," Maillol said, "and the breast she is holding will be like a flower." After which he showed me preparatory drawings that represented the work in its finished state.

"I should like," he added, "for this work to be more realistic, more alive than anything I have done until now. It is for that reason that I work this time with a model and not only from drawings, as I did previously. However, drawings are still a great help and I continue to make many of them. I should actually make thousands, from every conceivable angle, particularly for this figure, so that it will turn out the way I want it to be."

"Formerly I worked with much greater ease," he continued. "Take L'Action enchaînée, that enormous torso—well, I did that in ten days. In a fortnight all the essential part was finished, and the statue was entirely ready in three months. Today things are different; often I have to start all over as many as ten times, I change, I take off, I add . . . Or consider Flore (66) which I made without a model and without a drawing. For L'Action enchaînée I had my wife, but Flore is much taller and slimmer than she was, an altogether different body, and yet I fashioned her as though there was nothing to it."

While he thus spoke, Maillol had seated himself on a low chair in front of the statue. Seizing a small trowel, he picked up some wet plaster in a bowl and began working on the right leg. Unable to obtain the fine-grade plas-

ter he generally used, he now was forced to have recourse to ordinary mason's plaster of a greenish tint with which work was much less pleasant.

"Everything is horribly difficult," he stated. "I wonder how I am going to finish this statue, especially that leg which doesn't come along."

He shook his head just as there was a slight grating of the garden gate. "That is Dina, my model," he said. "She comes every day at two and poses until five o'clock when night begins to fall."

At these words a young, black-haired girl appeared in the door, rather small, with bare arms and legs, a crown of braids wound around her head, her face large and radiant. Happy to sense an interruption of the monotonous days, weeks and months during which she had posed for this work, she showed me all the sketches scattered on the sofa, relating for each under what circumstances it had been done. She was visibly proud to find herself in all these studies, to let me admire her back and her legs, her belly and her throat, for—before being works of art—these drawings to her were reflections of her buoyant loveliness. Then, with a few unembarrassed movements, she took off her blouse and skirt and soon appeared in splendid nudity. Her body, still tanned by the last rays of the previous summer, was full and round, bursting with health; in her slightly slit eyes, in her gestures, in her entire being there was something of the unconcern but also the savagery of a young animal. Her large shoulders, her round and firm breasts, her smooth belly, her rather flat back, the curve of her thighs, and her strong legs, all these somewhat stocky and muscular forms seemed to present only

It was an astounding spectacle: two naked girls side by side, related and yet dissimilar. . . .

. . . the great nude was left in all its dazzling whiteness on the hillside. . . . .

few analogies with the slender body of the statue. Standing next to the plaster, assuming the same attitude, inclining her head and casting down her eyes, gracefully lifting one hand to her shoulder and molding the other around her breast, Dina seemed to underline even further the difference between herself and Maillol's work.

It was an astounding spectacle: two naked girls side by side, related and yet dissimilar; a spectacle that made it possible to perceive clearly the transposition the artist had achieved. It became evident to what degree the model was but a guide for the sculptor and with what obstinacy he was pursuing a preconceived idea . . . one could almost say *in spite* of the harmonious forms this beautiful creature offered him. Indeed, Maillol was

gathering from the living source what information he needed, but even in his drawings made specifically for this work he had elongated all proportions. Moreover, among the many recent studies I had seen, there were also a few older ones that he had found useful.

As though he guessed what I was thinking, Maillol explained: "The further one gets away from nature, the more one becomes an artist; the closer one sticks to it, the uglier the work becomes. That is the problem: should one copy nature and produce things that resemble direct casts, or should one turn one's back to it as do the Africans in their primitive sculpture?"

Leaving Maillol to his work, I went down to the beach and on to a slope with cacti and cypresses, on the top of which stood the large wooden shed where I expected to find *L'Air*,

finally terminated and temporarily abandoned to its fate. But a recent storm had carried its shelter away and the great nude was left in all its dazzling whiteness on the hillside, silhouetted against the mountains amid vines and pine trees. Majestic and aerial at the same time, *L'Air* seemed enthroned in this magnificent setting as though it had been conceived for it. And slowly dusk spread its veil over the gorgeous body.

The next morning, a bag with provisions dangling from his shoulder, Maillol came to call for me at the inn and then rushed to alert Dina who was going to join us without his wife's knowledge. Accepting the girl's presence only with the greatest difficulty, Madame Maillol did not tolerate that their relationship extend beyond the artist's studio. She must not

27

A few more steps and we were in front of Maillol's simple farmhouse. . . .

find out, he sheeplishly explained, that Dina would come with us to his small farm.

It was a splendid morning. A clear March sun shone from the cloudless sky, a slight breeze shook the almond-trees, and the camelias were sparkling among green-black leaves. Having refused many times my help, Maillol finally let me carry his bag, though he insisted on keeping the gourd . . . and we were on our way. In passing he pointed out the house where Wanda Landowska had taken refuge.

"I go there frequently when she is alone," he said. "The first times I attended her practice sessions, I found it rather difficult to listen to the same musical phrase repeated endlessly, but soon I could distinguish the almost imperceptible progress she was making. Little by little I understood how her interpretation was

influencing the score. Sometimes she even changed a note when the original text came out flat on her instrument . . . and I witnessed all that. I do not really understand much about music, I am merely sensitive to it, but Wanda Landowska made me appreciate and understand Bach. Thanks to this great artist I have spent marvellous moments."

We had left the last houses behind and passed a viaduct; soon the hamlet of old Banyuls appeared at our left and there, after a turn of the road, was Dina waiting for us. She too carried some supplies wrapped in paper. We continued our walk through the spring morning. The road undulated between slanting fields, scarcely shaded by young trees with timid foliage. From everywhere freshly tilled vineyards seemed to glide to our feet. The neat lines traced by rows of recently clipped plants

transformed this hilly landscape into a vast chessboard of irregular squares, enlivened here and there by some peach or almond trees whose petals were coloring the ground.

The artist was in an exuberant mood. As always, he was wearing an old suit of ribbed brown velvet, well-worn espadrilles, and his beret. One hand hooked to the lapel of his jacket, he was walking erect and fast. His lively eyes were smiling and his entire face lit up with joy whenever our exclamations flattered his filial pride in this region so meticulously ordered and at the same time so untamed. Keeping to the side of a brook, La Roume (usually dried out in the summer), we soon perceived to our right, though almost completely hidden by trees, a white building on the gentle slope that descended toward the water. A few more steps and we were in front of Maillol's simple farmhouse (*métairie*). Four steps separated the road from the garden where rosebushes, grass, cactus plants, fig trees, and wild flowers crowded a small terrace. At left was a perfect square of lawn, enclosed by three regular rows of cypresses, while the house bordered it on the fourth side, so that the spot was always in the shade. Maillol himself had planted these trees some forty years ago when he also had a covered veranda built along that side of the house; it extended into the interior this area of freshness and shade. But those were the only exterior changes which he made when he inherited the building, being anxious to preserve its rustic character. Inside, however, he had freely altered things to conform to his requirements. The lower part was occupied almost exclusively by a large kitchen, communicating with the small terrace in front of the house, whereas on the upper floor was a spacious studio, connected through a hallway with two small bedrooms.

Having opened all the shutters, Maillol turned the kitchen over to Dina who immediately began busying herself with dishes and pans. With a pitcher and a pail he went to fetch water in La Roume, then picked up a small axe and started cutting some dead wood for the kitchen fire. His lively and brisk movements did not show the slightest fatigue and he accomplished every task with an astonishing grace, as though—all his life—he had done nothing but fetch water and cut wood.

Then he took me through the garden. He spoke at length of all the plants, inspecting with special care the trees that had been affected by the exceptional rigors of the past winter. He was extremely unhappy to notice that one of the large pines of which he had been particularly proud was slowly dying. With sadness in his voice he said:

"Nature does help men a great deal, but often she destroys what she has created, for nature has no respect for herself."

We returned to the brook to water four tiny fig trees that the artist—according to an old local custom—had planted on Ash Wednesday. With infinite tenderness he bent over the shoots to see whether they had taken root. What a sight to watch the tall old man take care of young plants whose fruit he might not live to gather! But the thought of a limited future did not seem ever to cross his mind; in whatever he did or said there never was the slightest restriction as to the years ahead; he spoke of them with the certainty of one who would see them. Not once did this man, who was going on eighty, allude to death; quite to the contrary, he seemed to be full of hope and acted like someone still at the dawn of his life. It was this attitude that allowed him to calmly concentrate on his work, neither hurried nor preoccupied with the final curtain.

While watering the young fig shoots, he explained not only how the sun and the reflection of a nearby wall would hasten their growth, but also held forth on the specific taste of their fruit since he had selected a particularly savory variety. Then he scrutinized the sky for the direction of the wind and predicted the weather. From the position of the sun he noticed that the time for lunch had come.

A table and chairs had already been installed on the terrace. Soon Dina brought out a dish of mussels prepared *à l'espagnole*, that is cooked in rice with curry and saffron. Maillol began to fill our glasses with the wine he had carried in the gourd. The sun was shining brightly, the food was spicy, the wine mellow, and the water fresh and cool. For desert Maillol produced from his pocket some oranges and candied fruit.

Afterward he lit his pipe which he smoked only once a day and began speaking of the summer of 1940, spent entirely at this farmhouse. He had lived there alone because his wife had refused to accompany him. Fortunately the heat had been much less than usual and he had thus been able to work without interruption. Dina had arrived every morning on foot from Banyuls, carrying provisions, and had left around five after preparing a soup for dinner. When it rained and she couldn't come, Maillol himself had cooked his frugal meal and spent the time reading, preferably the comedies of Aristophanes, the plays of Shakespeare or anthologies of poetry.

It had been a summer of work which reminded him of his youth when, living in seclusion with him, his wife had generously offered him her young beauty. Yet in 1940 he had not led, at the farmhouse, the life of a lover but rather the existence of an aged hermit, meditating in absolute isolation and contemplating, day after day, the body of a young girl that inspired his work. Dina had posed in the studio, on the veranda or on the lawn surrounded by cypresses. Most of the time she had thus lived like a happy savage, naked in the sun that gilded her body . . . a fact that drove Maillol to despair since he would have preferred, for his paintings, a clear and rosy skin.

As Dina retired to the kitchen, the artist showed me in the upstairs studio the oils on which he had worked during the summer, as well as the drawings. There were large canvases with decorative compositions and small, spontaneous oil sketches. As to the drawings, they were mostly very big, nudes of Dina with neat contours, precisely modeled but somehow lacking the intimate charm of his small and less ambitious studies.

Once everything had been cleaned up, we closed the shutters and doors and took to the road. We left before the twilight descended into the valleys. Dina soon parted to take another route. We reached the beach of Banyuls as the last rays of the sun began to color the sky.

The next morning we met on the beach to walk once more to the war memorial. After lunch I went for the last time to the studio where Maillol was working while expecting Dina. He was seated on his low chair in front of the statue, having near him a small washbasin with wet plaster; with his trowel he retouched the calf of the right leg.

"Frequently," he said, "the young girls of Banyuls are embarrassed when I seem to stare at their legs; they imagine I do not know what, yet I only look for information because this leg, on which my figure stands, is awfully difficult to do. The other one is child's play; I could make it with eyes closed, but this one: I add something and it looks well, then I turn the statue a little and it becomes impossible. I must take off what I have just added. That is because the eye cannot see the whole of a sculpture with one glance, so that one commits errors and only realizes this when examining the piece from a different angle. That is why I need so much information and why I must make so many drawings."

"Eventually you'll conquer those difficulties," I replied, "as you have always done in the past."

"Oh, don't say that," he retorted vividly. "Often there is something in my sculptures that didn't come off completely. Besides, one almost always finds a weak spot in a work of art, even in the finest statues of antiquity. As to my own, the difficulty lies invariably with the legs. The belly, the breasts, the back, they sometimes come all by themselves, but the legs . . . and yet they are what has always interested me most. In my drawings I manage to establish them well, in my sculpture, however, its different. . . ."

Saying this Maillol, with his long fingers, stroked the curve of the right leg, the ankle of which he had just made slightly thicker. But after slowly turning the statue, he picked up his small trowel and scraped the thin layer of plaster he had just added; the shape that had satisfied him in frontal view appeared faulty in profile. Untiringly he thus polished and repolished this leg which supported the weight of the young body, his tool producing imperceptible alterations, remindful of Wanda Landowska who, with the same obstinacy, achieved slow progress by patiently repeating the same chords.

The artist got up to stretch a little and spoke of the arms that soon were to complete this work. He pointed to the harmonious lines of throat, belly and hips which would later be hidden by the elbows, regretting openly that he would have to disrupt some of the most successful profiles of this figure.

"Greek statues," he said, "often are much more beautiful without arms because these always hide part of the body—either the bust or the stomach, or the waistline—which is absolutely marvelous and which we can admire today since the arms have disappeared. . . ."

Maillol stopped. Dina's steps could be heard in the garden. For three hours she would now pose and he would continue to polish the forms of the adolescent, as the sea polishes the pebbles it rolls ceaselessly. Although my presence seemed in no way to disturb them, I decided to leave.

It was my last afternoon in Banyuls. The next day the train would take me to Marseilles where I expected to embark. After dinner I walked up once more to the pink house to say farewell. I was expected; logs were burning in the huge fireplace, bottles and glasses were set on a large Spanish table. By the fire we chatted again about art and life. Maillol reminisced about the sculptures of Degas and about the artist himself, whom he had known as a very old man. Then he produced some poor photographs of the figure for the monument to Barbusse left behind at Marly where a young sculptor, Couturier, was finishing some secondary parts. Just as the piece he was now working on with Dina was the first executed with a model, this project for the first time showed a body in an agitated attitude. The sculpture was based on elements of *La Montagne*, cut apart and reassembled in a totally different fashion. It was eventually to become

La Rivière (106). But the photographs were too bad to allow closer inspection.

Maillol then played some records of Basque folk music, *Sardanas*, to which people dance wherever Catalan is spoken, from Barcelona to Perpignan. It is a music composed of variations of an initial theme, played by wind instruments—not unlike bagpipes—as well as by brass and drums. The captivating rhythms of these simple melodies prompted me to ask him what kind of steps were executed to these cadences. He rose and, with a smile, performed a Catalan *Sardana*. There, by the gleam of the fire, with little steps forward and backward almost on the point of his toes, slightly bending now to the right, now to the left, he moved with an amazing naturalness. Far from being ridiculous, his movements were proud and noble, his gestures sparse, even grave, and infinitely harmonious. Thus the tall old man with the white beard sketched dance steps in which his entire youth lived again. An indescribable joy spread over his wrinkled face, his eyes were laughing; he himself seemed surprised by the ease with which he could resurrect the movements of a dance that once had animated every local feast. Then, after indicating a reverence with the inclination of his head and a gesture of his hand, he sat down.

"You see," he said happily, "I still remember the rounds of my country."

It was getting late. We shook hands sadly. He accompanied me down the moonlit staircase and for the last time the grating gate of the garden was shut behind me.

Dina had promised to write but never did. Maillol's eightieth birthday was celebrated on December 8, 1941. The lecture that The Museum of Modern Art in New York had announced for that day was attended by exactly eight people. After Pearl Harbor all communications with France were suspended. Later, Dina was arrested but the artist managed to have her set free

Maillol continued to work. "The day when I can no longer work," he had told me, "I shall be dead." But in spite of his relentless efforts, the figure of the young girl which he had meant to call *La Rose* was never finished. Her name was changed to *L'Harmonie* (111). Her arms are still missing so that her exquisite lines flow uninterrupted, as in the broken statues of Antiquity.

The artist lived to see the liberation of Paris, but on September 15, 1944, after a visit to Dufy who had settled nearby, the car driven by his doctor met with an accident. Maillol's jaw was broken and he could not speak. Transported to a clinic run by nuns, he wrote down his last thoughts on a pupil's exercise book. At his request taken back to Banyuls, he died in the house where he was born, on September 27, 1944.

Since then Dina has watched over his work and over his posthumous fate. In 1964 she presented the French government with eighteen major bronzes of his, to be set up in the Tuileries Gardens, in the heart of Paris. There they now are surrounded by lawns and trees with the perspective of the Louvre in the background. Maillol, who had always admired the sculptures in the park of Versailles, would have loved it.

WORKS IN THE EXHIBITION   *Painting and Tapestry*

1

Self Portrait
(Portrait de l'artiste par lui-même). 1888

Oil on canvas, 12⅝ x 9⅜″ (32 x 24 cm.)

Not signed

Collection Dina Vierny, Paris

2

*Young Girl in Red (Portrait of Mlle. Sarrail)
(Fillette en rouge [Portrait de Mlle.
Sarrail]). 1888*

Oil on canvas, 58½ x 40" (148.5 x 101.5 cm.)

Signed l.r. "Aristide Maillol"

Private Collection

3

*Crowned Child
(L'Enfant couronné). 1890*

Oil on canvas, 18½ x 15¾" (47 x 40 cm.)

Not signed

Collection Dina Vierny, Paris

4

Bust of a Girl
(Buste de jeune fille). 1890
Oil on canvas, 21⅝ x 18⅛″ (55 x 46 cm.)
Not signed
Collection Dina Vierny, Paris

5

Two Young Girls
(Les Deux jeunes filles). c. 1890

Oil on canvas, 23¼ x 41¼″ (59 x 105 cm.)

Not signed

Collection Dina Vierny, Paris

6

Washerwomen
(Les Lavandières). 1893
Oil on canvas, 25¼ x 31½" (64 x 80 cm.)
Signed l.l. "A. MAILLOL"
Collection Paul Josefowitz, Switzerland

7

Portrait of Mme. Maillol
(Portrait de Mme. Maillol). 1894
Oil on canvas, 16½ x 12⅝" (42 x 32 cm.)
Not signed
Collection Dina Vierny, Paris

8

Tapestry (Tapisserie). 1894

Wool, 74¾ x 41⅜" (190 x 105 cm.)

Signed l.c. "Aristide Maillol"

Collection Dina Vierny, Paris

9

Project for a Tapestry for the Princess Bibesco
(Projet de tapisserie pour la Princesse
Bibesco). 1895 (recto)

Oil on canvas, 18¼ x 22″ (46.5 x 56 cm.)

Not signed

Collection Dina Vierny, Paris

10

Child's Swing
(L'Escarpolette). 1896
Oil on paperboard, 8⅝ x 10⅝″ (22 x 27 cm.)
Cartoon for a tapestry
Not signed
Collection Dina Vierny, Paris

11

Portrait of a Child
(Portrait d'enfant). 1898
Oil on wood, 13¾ x 11⅞″ (35 x 30 cm.)
Not signed
Collection Dina Vierny, Paris

12

Côte d'azur (The Mediterranean)
(La Côte d'azur [La Méditerranée]). c. 1898

Oil on canvas, 37¾ x 41⅜″ (96 x 105 cm.)

Not signed

Collection Musée du Petit Palais, Paris

13

Two Bathers
(Deux baigneuses). c. 1898
Oil on canvas, 38⅛ x 48″ (97 x 122 cm.)
Not signed
Collection Musée du Petit Palais, Paris

14

The Woman and The Wave
(La Femme et la vague). c. 1898
Oil on canvas, 21½ x 17½″ (54.5 x 44.5 cm.)
Signed l.r. "Aristide Maillol"
Pflueger Collection, New York

15

Portrait of Dina
(Portrait de Dina). 1940
Oil on canvas, 21⅝ x 18½″ (55 x 47 cm.)
Not signed
Collection Dina Vierny, Paris

16

Dina with a Silk Scarf
(Dina au foulard). 1941

Oil on canvas, 37⅜ x 43⅜" (95 x 110 cm.)

Not signed

Collection Dina Vierny, Paris

17

Two Girls in a Wood
(Les Deux jeunes filles dans un bois). 1942
Oil on wood, 8¼ x 13″ (21 x 33 cm.)
Signed l.r. with monogram
Collection Dina Vierny, Paris

18

Large Yellow Nude
(Le Grand nu jaune). 1943
Oil on canvas, 39⅜ x 24⅜″ (100 x 62 cm.)
Not signed
Collection Dina Vierny, Paris

Sculpture

19

Clothed Nabis
(Nabis habillé). 1895

Bronze, 8½" h. (21.5 cm.)

Cast no. 2/6

Signed with monogram; inscribed "Alexis Rudier
Fondeur, Paris;" "2/6"

Lent by Dominion Gallery, Montreal

20

The Couple
(Le Couple). 1896

Bronze, 6¾" h. (17 cm.)

Cast no. 4/6

Signed with monogram; inscribed "Alexis Rudier
Fondeur, Paris;" "4/6"

Collection Dina Vierny, Paris

21

Washerwoman
(La Lavandière). 1896

Bronze, 4½" h. (11.5 cm.)

Cast no. 1/6

Signed with monogram; inscribed "Alexis
Rudier Fondeur, Paris;" "1/6"

Collection The University of Michigan Museum
of Art, Purchase made possible by The Friends
of The Museum of Art

22

Bust of a Woman
(Buste de femme). 1898

Bronze, 12" h. (30.5 cm.)

Cast no. 5

Signed with monogram; stamped "CIRE C.
VALSUANI PERDUE;" "No. 5"

The Phillips Collection, Washington, D.C.

23

Clock
(La Pendule). 1899

Bronze, 20¼" h. (51.5 cm.)

Cast no. 5/6

Signed with monogram; inscribed "Alexis Rudier
Fondeur, Paris;" "5/6"

Lent by Perls Galleries, New York

24

Eve with an Apple
(Eve à la pomme). 1899

Bronze, 22⅝" h. (58 cm.)

No cast no.

Signed "Aristide Maillol;" inscribed "Alexis
Rudier Fondeur, Paris"

Private Collection

25

Torso of a Woman: Eve
(Torse de femme: Eve). 1900

Bronze, 17" h. (43.2 cm.)

Cast no. 1/6

Signed with monogram; inscribed "Alexis
Rudier Fondeur, Paris;" "1/6"

Lent by Perls Galleries, New York

26

Bather

(Baigneuse). 1900

Bronze, 48″ h. (122 cm.)

Cast no. 4/6

Signed "A. MAILLOL;" stamped "CIRE C. VALSUANI PERDUE;" "4/6"

Lent by Perls Galleries, New York

27

Crouching Girl

(Jeune fille accroupie). 1900

Bronze, 7¾″ h. (19.6 cm.)

No cast no.

Signed with monogram; inscribed "Alexis Rudier Fondeur, Paris"

Private Collection

28

Crouching Woman with Pointed Chignon
(Femme accroupie au chignon pointu). c. 1900

Bronze, 7" h. (17.8 cm.)

Cast no. 4/6

Signed with monogram; inscribed "Alexis Rudier
Fondeur, Paris;" "4/6"

Lent by Perls Galleries, New York

29

The Modest One
(La Pudique). 1900

Bronze, 6¾" h. (17.2 cm.)

Cast no. 2/6

Signed with monogram; inscribed "Alexis Rudier
Fondeur, Paris;" "2/6"

Collection C. B. Marcuse

30
Pensive One
(La Pensive). c. 1900
Terra cotta, 6⅛" h. (15.5 cm.)
Signed with monogram
Collection Albright-Knox Art Gallery, Buffalo,
New York, Gift of A. Conger Goodyear

31
First Study for "Air"
(Première étude pour "L'Air"). c. 1900
Terra cotta, 6" h. (15.2 cm.)
Not signed
Private collection

32

Seated Girl Covering her Eyes
(Jeune fille assise se voilant les yeux). 1900
Terra cotta, 8¼" h. (21 cm.)
Signed "ARISTIDE MAILLOL F"
Collection The Alex Hillman Family Foundation

33

Draped Torso
(Torse à la chemise). 1900
Plaster, 11" h (29 cm.), including base
Not signed or inscribed
Collection The Alex Hillman Family Foundation

34

Standing Bather, Drapery over Right Arm
(Baigneuse debout, drapé sur le bras droit).
1900

Bronze, 25" h. (63.5 cm.)

No cast no.

Signed "Aristide Maillol;" inscribed "A. BINGEN
et COSTENOBLE Fondeurs, Paris"

Collection Mr. and Mrs. Alexandre Rosenberg,
New York

35

Standing Bather
(Baigneuse debout). c. 1900

Bronze, 26⅜" h. (67 cm.)

Unknown cast no. of edition of 6

Signed "Aristide Maillol;" inscribed "Alexis
Rudier Fondeur, Paris"

Lent by Paul Drey Gallery, New York

36

Two Female Wrestlers
(Les Deux lutteuses). 1900

Bronze, 7¼" h. (18.4 cm.)

Cast no. 4/6

Signed with monogram; inscribed "J Godard
Fondeur Paris;" "4/6"

Lent by Perls Galleries, New York

Another cast is illustrated

37

Seated Girl Holding her Leg
(Jeune fille assise, tenant la jambe). c. 1900

Terra cotta, 8½″ h. (21.5 cm.)

Not signed or inscribed

Ex collection Mary Cassatt

Collection Mrs. Percy C. Madeira

38

Seated Girl Holding her Leg
(Jeune fille assise, tenant la jambe). c. 1900

Bronze, 9″ h. (23 cm.)

Cast no. 6/6

Signed with monogram; inscribed
"CIRE C. VALSUANI PERDUE;" "6/6"

Lent by Paul Rosenberg & Co., New York

39
Leda
(*Léda*). c. 1900
Terra cotta, 10¾″ h. (27.3 cm.)
Signed with monogram
Private Collection

40
Leda
(*Léda*). c. 1900
Bronze, 11½″ h. (29.2 cm.)
Cast no. 1/6
Signed with monogram; inscribed "Alexis Rudier
Fondeur, Paris"
Lent by Paul Rosenberg & Co., New York

41

Kneeling Girl, without Arms
(La Jeune fille agenouillé, sans bras). 1900

Bronze, 33" h. (83.8 cm.)

Cast no. 1/2 of edition of 4

Signed "A. Maillol;" inscribed "Alexis Rudier
Fondeur, Paris;" "1/2"

Collection San Francisco Museum of Art, Gift of
Hans G. M. de Schulthess and Amalia Loew de
Schulthess in memory of Alexandre Rabow,
San Francisco

42

Kneeling Girl
(La Jeune fille agenouillé). 1902

Bronze, 6⅝″ h. (17.5 cm.)

No cast no.

Not signed or inscribed

Collection Mr. and Mrs. David Lloyd Kreeger

43

Night

(La Nuit). 1902-09

Bronze, 41¼" h. (105 cm.)

Cast no. 4

Signed with monogram; inscribed "Alexis Rudier
Fondeur, Paris;" "No. 4"

Collection The Metropolitan Museum of Art,
Gift of Maurice Wertheim, 1950

44
Night
(La Nuit). 1902
Terra cotta, 7⅛" h. (18 cm.)
Signed with monogram
Collection Mrs. Henry F. Fischbach

45
Study for "Night"
(Etude pour "La Nuit"). c. 1908
Bronze, 6⅞" h. (17.5 cm.)
No cast no.
Signed with monogram; inscribed "Alexis Rudier Fondeur, Paris"
Collection Mr. Robert Mezbourian, Paris

46

The Mediterranean
(La Méditerranée). 1902-05

Bronze, 41" h. (104 cm.)

No cast no.

Signed with monogram; inscribed "Alexis Rudier Fondeur, Paris"

Collection The Museum of Modern Art, New York, Gift of Stephen C. Clark, 1953

47

Study for "The Mediterranean"
(Etude pour "La Méditerranée"). c. 1902

Bronze, 7" h. (17.8 cm.)

Cast no. 1/6

Signed with monogram; inscribed "Alexis Rudier Fondeur, Paris;" "1/6"

Lent by Perls Galleries, New York

48

Study for "The Mediterranean"
(Etude pour "La Méditerranée"). c. 1905

Bronze, 25½" h. (64.2 cm.)

Cast no. 6/6

Signed with monogram; inscribed "Alexis Rudier Fondeur, Paris;" "6/6"

Collection Mr. and Mrs. Charles Wohlstetter

49
Thought
(La Pensée). 1902-05
Terra cotta, 7″ h. (17.8 cm.)
Signed with monogram
Collection Mrs. Henry F. Fischbach

50
Crouching Woman
(Femme accroupie). 1904-05
Bronze relief, 39 x 40¾ x 4⅛″
(99.1 x 103.5 x 10.5 cm.)
Cast no. 1/6
Signed with monogram; stamped "CIRE C.
VALSUANI PERDUE;" "1/6"
Lent by Dominion Gallery, Montreal

51

Desire
(*Le Désir*). 1906-08

Plaster relief, 46⅞ x 45 x 7¼"
(119 x 114.3 x 18.4 cm.)

Not signed

Collection The Museum of Modern Art, New
York, Gift of the artist, 1930

52

Action in Chains, Monument to Louis-Auguste Blanqui

(L'Action enchaînée, Monument à Louis-Auguste Blanqui). 1906

Bronze, 84½" h. (214.5 cm.)

Cast no. 6/6

Signed with monogram; inscribed "Georges Rudier Fondeur, Paris;" "6/6"

Collection Dina Vierny, Paris

53

Torso of "Action in Chains"
(Torse de "L'Action enchaînée"). 1905

Bronze, 51¼" h. (130.2 cm.)

Cast no. 1/6

Signed with monogram; stamped "CIRE C. VALSUANI PERDUE;" "1/6"

Private collection

54
Study for "Action in Chains," without Arms
(Etude pour "L'Action enchaînée," sans bras).
1905-06

Bronze, 12½" h. (31.8 cm.)

Cast no. 1/6

Signed with monogram; inscribed "Alexis Rudier
Fondeur, Paris;" "1/6"

Lent by Paul Rosenberg & Co., New York

55
Small Torso of "Action in Chains"
(Petite torse de "L'Action enchaînée"). 1905

Bronze, 5½" h. (14 cm.)

Cast no. 2/6

Signed with monogram; inscribed "Alexis Rudier
Fondeur, Paris;" "2/6"

Collection Dr. and Mrs. A. D. Herschberg, Paris

56

Small Seated Woman with Chignon
(Petite femme assise au chignon). 1905

Bronze, 7" h. (17.8 cm.)

Cast no. 5/6

Signed with monogram; inscribed "Alexis Rudier
Fondeur, Paris;" "5/6"

Lent by Perls Galleries, New York

57

Woman with Dove
(Femme à la colombe). 1905

Bronze, 10" h. (25.4 cm.)

Cast no. 3

Signed with monogram; inscribed "Alexis Rudier
Fondeur, Paris;" "3"

Lent by Perls Galleries, New York

58

Standing Bather with Drapery
(Baigneuse debout drapée). c. 1905

Terra cotta, 11" h. (28 cm.)

Signed with monogram

Collection Mr. and Mrs. Alexandre Rosenberg,
New York

59

Seated Woman (Painted by Renoir)
(Femme assise [peinte par Renoir]). 1907

Bronze, 8⅛" h. (20.6 cm.)

Cast no. 1/6

Signed "Aristide Maillol;" inscribed "J Godard
Fondeur Paris;" "1/6"

Lent by Perls Galleries, New York

60

Head of Renoir
(Tête de Renoir). 1907

Bronze, 16⅛" h. (41 cm.)

No cast no.

Signed with monogram; inscribed "Alexis Rudier
Fondeur, Paris"

Collection Mr. and Mrs. Joseph S. Wohl

61

Young Cyclist
(Jeune cycliste). 1907

Bronze, 38" h. (96.5 cm.)

No cast no.

Signed with monogram; inscribed "Alexis Rudier
Fondeur, Paris"

Collection Fogg Art Museum, Harvard University,
Cambridge, Massachusetts, Purchase-Friends of
the Fogg and Alpheus Hyatt Funds

62

Torso on a Dolphin
(Torse sur le dauphin). c. 1910

Bronze, 6¾" h. (17.1 cm.)

Cast no. 9

Signed with monogram; stamped "CIRE C.
VALSUANI PERDUE;" "No. 9"

Collection Deborah Weyhe Dennis/Weyhe
Gallery

63

Pomona with Raised Arms
(Pomone aux bras levés). 1910

Bronze, 64½″ h. (163.9 cm.)

No cast no.

Signed with monogram; inscribed "Alexis Rudier
Fondeur, Paris"

Collection Mr. and Mrs. David Lloyd Kreeger

The following four works, *Pomona, Flora, Spring*
and *Summer,* together form the group *The Seasons*
(Les Saisons).

64

Summer
(L'Eté). 1910-11

Bronze, 64" h. (162.5 cm.)

No cast no.

Signed "A. Maillol"

Lent by Wildenstein & Company, New York

65

Spring
(Le Printemps). 1910-11

Bronze, 66" h. (67.6 cm.)

No cast no.

Signed "A. Maillol;" inscribed "CIRE C. VALSUANI PERDUE"

Collection The Museum of Modern Art, New York, Gift of Mr. and Mrs. Alexandre P. Rosenberg, 1974

66

Flora
(La Flore). 1911

Bronze, 66″ h. (167.5 cm.)

No cast no.

Signed with monogram; inscribed "Alexis Rudier
Fondeur, Paris"

Collection Mr. and Mrs. Nathan Smooke

67

Flora, Nude
(La Flore, nue). 1910

Bronze, 67″ h. (170 cm.)

Cast no. 5/6

Signed with monogram; stamped "CIRE C.
VALSUANI PERDUE;" "5/6"

Lent by Perls Galleries, New York

68

Small Flora, Nude
(Petite Flore, nue). 1911

Bronze, 24″ h. (61 cm.)

Cast no. 2/6

Signed with monogram; inscribed "Alexis Rudier
Fondeur, Paris;" "2/6"

Private Collection, Paris

69

Spring, without Arms and Head
(Le Printemps sans bras et tête). c. 1910

Plaster, 58¼″ h. (148 cm.)

Signed "A. Maillol"

Collection The Metropolitan Museum of Art,
Marquand Fund, 1951; from The Museum of
Modern Art, gift of the Sculptor

70

Study for "Monument to Cézanne"
(Etude pour "Monument à Cézanne"). 1912-25

Bronze, 7" h. (17.8 cm.)

Cast no. 4/6

Signed "A. MAILLOL;" stamped "CIRE C. VALSUANI PERDUE;" "4/6"

Lent by Perls Galleries, New York

71

Study for "Monument to Cézanne," with Drapery
(Etude pour "Monument à Cézanne," drapée).
1912-25

Bronze, 9⅛" h. (23 cm.)

Cast no. 2/6

Signed with monogram; inscribed "Alexis Rudier Fondeur, Paris;" "2/6"

Lent by Paul Drey Gallery, New York

72

Venus without Necklace
(Vénus sans collier). 1918-28

Bronze, 69⅛" h. (175.5 cm.)

No cast no.

Signed with monogram; inscribed "Alexis Rudier
Fondeur, Paris"

Collection National Gallery of Art, Washington,
D.C., Ailsa Mellon Bruce Fund, 1965

73

Bather with a Scarf
(Baigneuse à l'écharpe). 1919

Bronze, 13⅜" h. (34 cm.)

Cast no. 4/6

Signed with monogram; inscribed "Alexis Rudier
Fondeur, Paris;" "4/6"

Collection Mr. and Mrs. Robert Zell,
Bloomfield Hills

74

Standing Woman Arranging her Hair
(Femme debout se coiffant). 1919-20

Bronze, 14¼" h. (36.2 cm.)

Cast no. 3/6

Signed with monogram; inscribed "Alexis Rudier
Fondeur, Paris;" "3/6"

Lent by Harold Diamond, Inc., New York

75

Young Standing Bather (Bather, Cladel)
(Jeune baigneuse debout [Baigneuse Cladel]).
1920

Bronze, 13" h. (33 cm.)

Cast no. 5/6

Signed with monogram; inscribed "Alexis Rudier
Fondeur, Paris;" "5/6"

Lent by Harold Diamond, Inc., New York

76

Standing Bather Arranging her Hair, Elbow Raised
(Baigneuse debout, se coiffant, coude levé).
1921

Bronze, 11¼" h. (28.5 cm.)

Cast no. 5/6

Signed with monogram; inscribed "Alexis Rudier Fondeur, Paris;" "5/6"

Lent by Harold Diamond Inc., New York

77

Large Seated Woman
(Grand femme assise). 1920-21

Bronze, 11¾" h. (29.8 cm.)

Cast no. 3/6

Signed with monogram; inscribed "Alexis Rudier Fondeur, Paris;" "3/6"

Private Collection

78

Woman with Thorn
(Femme à l'épine). 1920

Bronze, 6⅞" h. (17.2 cm.)

Cast no. 1/6

Signed with monogram; inscribed "Alexis Rudier Fondeur, Paris;" "1/6"

Lent by Perls Galleries, New York

79

Woman with Thorn
(Femme à l'épine). 1920

Terra cotta, 7″ h. (17.8 cm.)

Signed with monogram

Collection Mr. and Mrs. Alexandre Rosenberg,
New York

80

Holding Both Feet
(Se tenant les deux pieds). c. 1920

Bronze, 7½″ h. (18.4 cm.)

Cast no. 6/6

Signed with monogram; inscribed "Alexis Rudier
Fondeur, Paris;" "6/6"

Lent by Perls Galleries, New York

81

Holding One Foot
(Se tenant le pied). 1920-21

Bronze, 7½″ h. (18.4 cm.)

Cast no. 1/6

Signed with monogram; inscribed "Alexis Rudier
Fondeur, Paris;" "1/6"

Lent by Perls Galleries, New York

Torso of "Ile de France"
(Torse de "L'Ile de France"). 1921

Bronze, 47½" h. (120.6 cm.)

Cast no. 5/6

Signed with monogram; inscribed "Alexis Rudier
Fondeur, Paris;" "5/6"

Collection The Fine Arts Museums of San
Francisco, Mildred Anna Williams Fund Purchase

83

Ile de France.
(L'Ile de France). 1925

Bronze, 66" h. (167.5 cm.)

Cast no. 4

Signed with monogram; inscribed "Alexis Rudier
Fondeur, Paris;" "No. 4"

Lent by Wildenstein & Company, New York

84

Heroic Head (for Port Vendres Monument)
(Tête heroique [pour le monument de Port
Vendres]). 1923

Bronze, 23" h. (58.5 cm.)

Cast no. 6/6

Signed with monogram; inscribed "CIRE C.
VALSUANI PERDUE;" "6/6"

Lent by Perls Galleries, New York

85

Small Marie
(Petite Marie). 1925

Bronze, 26¾" h. (68 cm.)

Cast no. 2/6

Signed with monogram; inscribed "Alexis Rudier
Fondeur, Paris;" "2/6"

Private Collection, Paris

86

Marie. 1931

Bronze, 62¼" h. (158 cm.)

Cast no. 2

Signed with monogram; inscribed "Alexis Rudier
Fondeur, Paris;" "No. 2"

Collection Mrs. Rachel Adler Conkright, Caracas

87

Bather with Raised Arms
(La Baigneuse aux bras levés). 1930

Bronze, 31½" h. (80 cm.)

No cast no.; artist's cast, 6 other casts exist

Signed with monogram; inscribed "Alexis Rudier
Fondeur, Paris"

Collection Mr. and Mrs. Gene Lo Bell,
Great Neck, New York

88

Bather with Raised Arms
(La Baigneuse aux bras levés). 1930

Bronze, 63" h. (160 cm.)

Cast no. 6/6

Signed with monogram; inscribed "Alexis Rudier
Fondeur, Paris;" "6/6"

Lent by Perls Galleries, New York

89

Monument to Debussy
(Monument à Debussy). 1930

Bronze, 36¼" h. (91.5 cm.)

Cast no. 5/6

Signed "A. MAILLOL;" inscribed "Alexis Rudier
Fondeur, Paris;" "5/6"

Collection Evelyn Sharp

90

Study for "Monument to Debussy"
(Etude pour "Monument à Debussy"). 1930

Bronze, 12" h. (30.5 cm.)

Cast no. 5/6

Signed with monogram; inscribed "Alexis Rudier
Fondeur, Paris;" "5/6"

Collection Evelyn Sharp

91

Study for "Monument to Debussy"
(Etude pour "Monument à Debussy"). 1930

Bronze, 9½" h. (24 cm.)

Cast no. 3/6

Signed with monogram; inscribed "Alexis Rudier
Fondeur, Paris;" "3/6"

Private Collection, Cambridge, Massachusetts

92

Crouching Bather
(Baigneuse accroupie). 1930
Terra cotta, 5½″ h. (13.4 cm.)
Signed with monogram
Collection Mrs. Henry F. Fischbach

93

Crouching Bather, Moveable Base
(Baigneuse accroupie, socle mobile). 1930
Bronze, 6½″ h. (16.5 cm.)
No cast no.; artist's cast, 6 other casts exist
Signed with monogram; inscribed "Alexis Rudier
Fondeur, Paris"
Collection Dina Vierny, Paris

94
Thought
(Pensée). 1930
Bronze, 11″ h. (27.9 cm.)
Cast no. 1/6
Signed with monogram; inscribed "Alexis Rudier Fondeur, Paris;" "1/6"
Lent by Perls Galleries, New York

95
Seated Bather
(Baigneuse assise). 1930
Marble, 11″ h. (28 cm.)
Signed with monogram
Collection Dina Vierny, Paris

96

Two Girls
(*Les Deux jeunes filles*). 1930

Stone relief, 48 x 49″ (122 x 124.5 cm.)

Signed with monogram

Private collection

97

Three Nymphs
(Trois nymphes). 1930-37

Bronze, 62″ h. (157.5 cm.)

No cast no.; artist's proof

Signed with monogram; inscribed by the artist
"épr d'Arte;" inscribed "Alexis Rudier Fondeur,
Paris"

Collection The Minneapolis Institute of Arts,
The Ethel Morrison Van Derlip Fund

98

Mountain

(La Montagne). 1937

Lead, 65″ h. (165 cm.)

Cast no. 4/6

Signed "Aristide Maillol." inscribed "Georges
Rudier Fondeur, Paris;" "4/6"

Collection Dina Vierny, Paris

Another cast is illustrated

99

Study for "Mountain"

(Etude pour "La Montagne"). 1936

Bronze, 10⅝″ h. (27 cm.)

Cast no. 1/6

Signed with monogram; inscribed, "Alexis Rudier
Fondeur, Paris;" "1/6"

Lent by Perls Galleries, New York

100

France
(La France). 1936

Bronze, 24″ h. (61 cm.)

Cast no. 2/6

Signed "A. Maillol;" inscribed "Alexis Rudier
Fondeur, Paris;" "2/6"

Lent by Paul Drey Gallery, New York

101

Standing Woman, Arranging her Hair
(Nu debout, se coiffant). c. 1936

Bronze, 13¾″ h. (35 cm.)

Cast no. 1

Signed with monogram; inscribed "Alexis Rudier
Fondeur, Paris;" "No. I"

Collection The Metropolitan Museum of Art,
Edith Perry Chapman Fund, 1951, from The
Museum of Modern Art, gift of Abby Aldrich
Rockefeller

102

Seated Bather, Arranging her Hair (Dina)
(Baigneuse assise, se coiffant [Dina]). 1937.

Bronze, 8½" h. (21.5 cm.)

Cast no. 4

Signed with monogram; inscribed "Alexis Rudier
Fondeur, Paris;" "No. 4"

Lent by Perls Galleries, New York

103

Dina, Moveable Base
(Dina, socle-mobile). 1937

Bronze, 8" h. (20.3 cm.)

Cast no. 4/6

Signed with monogram; inscribed, "Alexis Rudier
Fondeur, Paris;" "4/6"

Collection Mr. and Mrs. Klaus G. Perls, New York

104

Seated Bather, Arranging her Hair
(Baigneuse assise, se coiffant). c. 1937

Terra cotta, 7" h. (17.8 cm.)

Signed with monogram

Collection Mr. and Mrs. Alexandre Rosenberg,
New York

105

Pomona with Lowered Arms; Pomona with Apples II
(Pomone aux bras tombants; La Pomone aux pommes II). 1937

Bronze, 65¾" h. (167 cm.)

Cast no. ?/4

Signed with monogram; inscribed "Alexis Rudier Fondeur, Paris"

Collection The Solomon R. Guggenheim Museum, New York

106

The River
(La Rivière). 1938-43

Lead, 53¾ x 90" (136.5 x 228.5 cm.)

Cast no. 2

Signed "A. Maillol;" inscribed "Alexis Rudier
Fondeur, Paris;" "No. 2"

Collection The Museum of Modern Art, New
York, Mrs. Simon Guggenheim Fund, 1949

107
Air
(*L'Air*). 1938
Lead, 55 x 100½" (139.7 x 255.3 cm.)
No cast no.; 1 of 2 artist's casts, 6 other casts exist
Signed with monogram; inscribed "Georges
Rudier Fondeur, Paris"
Collection Dina Vierny, Paris
Another cast is illustrated

108
Dina. 1940
Bronze, 13⅜" h. (34 cm.)
Cast no. 4/6
Signed with monogram; stamped "CIRE C.
VALSUANI PERDUE;" "4/6"
Private Collection, California

109
Dina. 1940-44
Marble, 13⅜" h. (34 cm.)
Signed with monogram
Collection Dina Vierny, Paris

110

Torso of Dina
(Torse de Dina). 1943

Bronze, 48¾" h. (124 cm.)

Cast no. 3/6

Signed with monogram; stamped "CIRE C.
VALSUANI PERDUE;" "3/6"

Lent by Perls Galleries, New York

111

Harmony
(L'Harmonie) 1944

Bronze, 60" h. (152.5 cm.)

Cast no. 3/6

Signed with monogram; stamped "CIRE C.
VALSUANI PERDUE;" "3/6"

Lent by Perls Galleries, New York

Drawing

112

Study of Head of a Girl
(Etude d'une tête de jeune fille). 1894
Charcoal on light tan paper, 13⅜ x 11″
(34 x 28 cm.)
Signed l.l. with monogram
Collection Dina Vierny, Paris

113

Woman
(Femme). 1894
Charcoal on gray paper, 9⅝ x 6⅝″ (25 x 17.5 cm.)
Signed l.r. with monogram
Collection Dina Vierny, Paris

114
Profile of a Woman
(Femme de profil). 1896
Pastel on gray wrapping paper, 13⅜ x 18⅛″
(34 x 46 cm.)
Signed l.l. with monogram
Collection Dina Vierny, Paris

115
Self Portrait
(Autoportrait). 1898 (recto)
Ink on gray-blue paper, 11⅜ x 8¼″ (29 x 21 cm.)
Not signed
Collection Dina Vierny, Paris

116

The Wave
(La Vague). 1898

Sanguine on tan paper, 10 x 10″ (25.2 x 25.2 cm.)

Signed l.r. with monogram

Collection Dina Vierny, Paris

117

Mme. Maillol in her Bath
(Mme. Maillol dans son bain). 1898

Charcoal on light gray paper, 11¾ x 7⅛″
(30 x 18 cm.)

Signed l.r. with monogram

Collection Dina Vierny, Paris

118

Study of a Man for the Relief "Desire"
(Etude de l'homme pour le relief "Le Désir")
1905

Pencil on gray wrapping paper, 10⅝ x 7⅞"
(27 x 20 cm.)

Signed l.r. with monogram

Collection Dina Vierny, Paris

119

Young Man
(Jeune homme). 1907

Sanguine and white chalk on ochre butcher's
paper, 14½ x 10⅝" (37 x 27 cm.)

Signed l.r. with monogram

Collection Dina Vierny, Paris

120

Desire
(Le Désir). 1908
Pastel on butcher's paper, 7⅞ x 8⅝″ (20 x 22 cm.)
Signed l.r. with monogram
Collection Dina Vierny, Paris

121

Mme. Maillol from the Back
(Mme. Maillol de dos). 1915
Sanguine on hand-made paper with artist's
watermark, 10¼ x 8¼″ (26 x 21 cm.)
Signed l.r. with monogram
Collection Dina Vierny, Paris

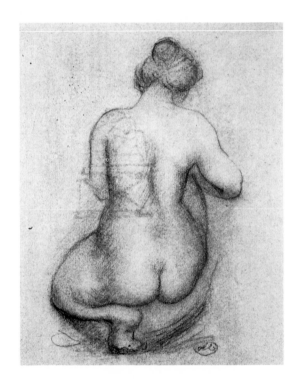

122

Girl Weeding
(La Jeune fille aux herbes). 1920
Sanguine on hand-made paper, 10⅜ x 13″
(26.5 x 33 cm.)
Signed l.r. with monogram
Collection Dina Vierny, Paris

123

Storm
(L'Orage). 1920
Charcoal on hand-made paper, 13⅛ x 9″
(33.5 x 23 cm.)
Not signed
Collection Dina Vierny, Paris

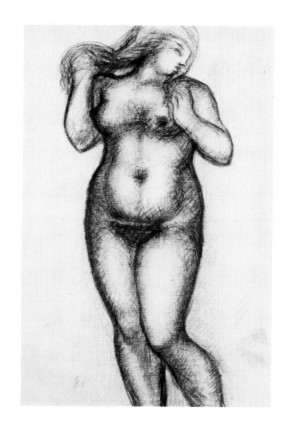

124

Ten Sketchbook Pages. 1921

Pencil on notebook paper, various sizes

Collection Dina Vierny, Paris

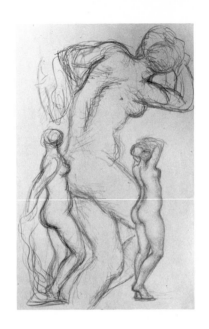

  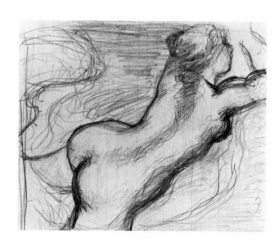

125

*Draped Bather
(Baigneuse drapée)*. 1921

Charcoal on hand-made paper, 12⅝ x 8⅝"
(32 x 22 cm.)

Signed l.r. with monogram

Collection Dina Vierny, Paris

126

*Nymph
(La Nymphe)*. 1921

Sanguine on hand-made paper, 11⅜ x 7⅛"
(29 x 18 cm.)

Signed l.r. with monogram

Collection Dina Vierny, Paris

127

*Woman Walking in the Water (Study for "Ile
de France")
(Femme marchant dans l'eau [Etude pour
"L' Ile de France"])*. 1921

Charcoal on butcher's paper, 15 x 9½"
(38 x 24 cm.)

Signed l.r. with monogram

Collection Dina Vierny, Paris

128

Seated Girl with Bent Knee
(Jeune Fille assise, genou levé). 1922
Sanguine on hand-made paper, 13 x 9⅝"
(33 x 24.5 cm.)
Signed l.l. with monogram
Collection Dina Vierny, Paris

129

Study for "Ile de France" (Movement)
(Etude pour "L'Ile de France" [mouvement]).
1923
Sanguine on hand-made paper, 13⅜ x 9¼"
(34 x 23.5 cm.)
Signed l.r. with monogram
Collection Dina Vierny, Paris

130

Woman from the back
(Femme de dos). 1925
Charcoal on white paper, 10⅝ x 7⅛"
(27 x 18 cm.)
Signed l.r. with monogram
Collection Dina Vierny, Paris

131

Earth
(La Terre). 1925
Sanguine on hand-made paper, 12¼ x 9⅜"
(31 x 24 cm.)
Signed l.r. with monogram
Collection Dina Vierny, Paris

132

Girl by the River
(Jeune fille à la rivière). 1925
Pastel on butcher's paper, 14¼ x 9½"
(36 x 24 cm.)
Signed l.r. with monogram
Collection Dina Vierny, Paris

133

Standing Nude, Facing Front
(Nu debout de face). 1925

Charcoal on light blue paper, 11⅝ x 8⅛″
(29.5 x 20.5 cm.)

Not signed

Collection Dina Vierny, Paris

134

Standing Woman
(Femme debout). 1925

Charcoal on paper, 12¼ x 5¾″ (31.2 x 14.7 cm.)

Not signed

Collection Dina Vierny, Paris

135

The Dreamer
(La Rêveuse). 1925

Sanguine on hand-made paper, 12½ x 9¼″
(31.6 x 23.5 cm.)

Signed l.l. with monogram

Collection Dina Vierny, Paris

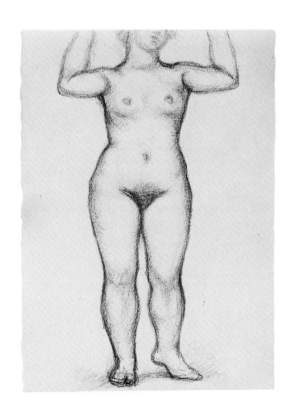

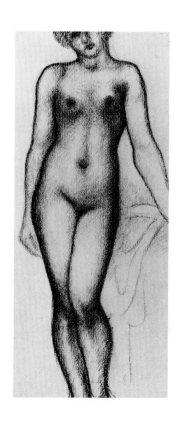

136

The Weed Picker
(La Ramasseuse d'herbes). 1925
Pastel on butcher's paper, 9¼ x 13⅜″
(23.5 x 34 cm.)
Signed l.r. with monogram
Collection Dina Vierny, Paris

137

Woman Walking with White Drapery
(La Femme qui marche à la draperie blanche).
1925
Pastel on butcher's paper, 14¾ x 9½″
(37.5 x 24 cm.)
Not signed
Collection Dina Vierny, Paris

138

*Woman Walking in the Water
(Femme marchant dans l'eau).* 1925

Charcoal on light tan paper, 10¼ x 6¼"
(26 x 16 cm.)

Not signed

Collection Dina Vierny, Paris

139

*Young Man, Facing Front
(Le Jeune homme de face).* 1925

Sanguine on hand-made paper, 15 x 5⅞"
(38 x 15 cm.)

Signed l.r. with monogram

Collection Dina Vierny, Paris

140

Thérèse. 1928

Drawing for lithograph for Ovid's *The Art
of Love*

Charcoal on light gray paper, 15⅜ x 12⅝"
(39 x 32 cm.)

Signed l.r. with monogram

Collection Dina Vierny, Paris

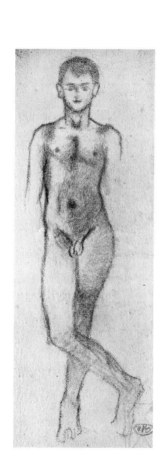

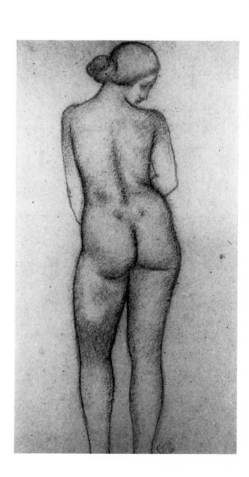

141

The Art of Love
(*L'Art d'aimer*). 1928
Charcoal on butcher's paper, 10⅝ x 9″
(27 x 23 cm.)
Not signed
Collection Dina Vierny, Paris

142

The Back of Thérèse
(*Le Dos de Thérèse*). 1929
Charcoal on hand-made paper, 28¾ x 21⅝″
(73 x 55 cm.)
Signed l.r. with monogram
Collection Dina Vierny, Paris

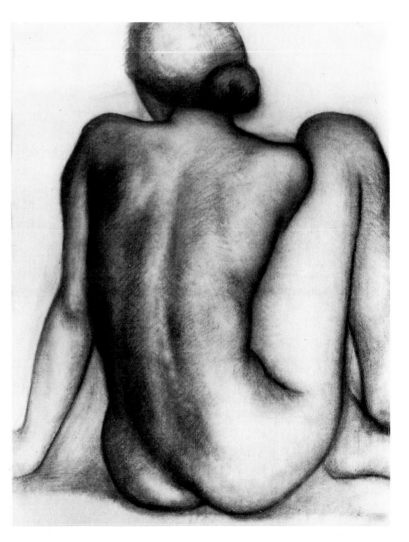

143

Back of Seated Woman (Drawing for "The Debussy")
(Dos assise [Dessin pour "Le Debussy"]).
1930
Charcoal on hand-made paper, 31 x 21½"
(78.5 x 54.5 cm.)
Not signed
Collection Dina Vierny, Paris

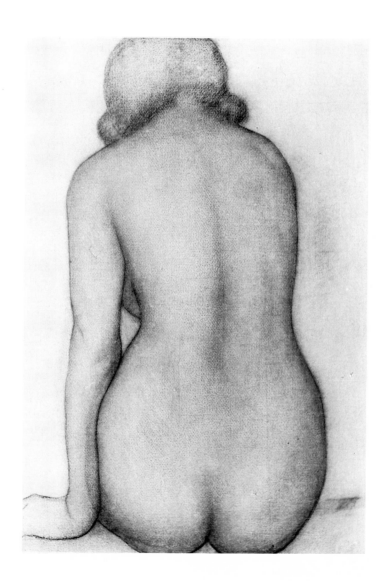

144

Woman with Crab
(Femme au crabe). 1930

Pencil and ink on gray paper, 7¾ x 8½"
(19.5 x 21.5 cm.)

Signed l.r. with monogram

Collection Dina Vierny, Paris

145

The Art of Love
(L'Art d'aimer). 1930

First drawing for lithographs for
Ovid's *The Art of Love*

Sanguine on butcher's paper, 15⅜ x 9⅞"
(39 x 25 cm.)

Signed l.r. with monogram

Collection Dina Vierny, Paris

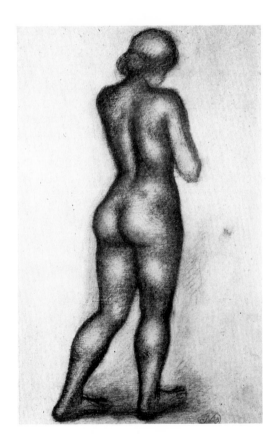

146

*Large Standing Nude from the Back
(Grand dos debout)*. 1930

Charcoal and white chalk on gray wrapping
paper, 46½ x 23⅞″ (118 x 60.5 cm.)

Signed l.r. with monogram

Collection Dina Vierny, Paris

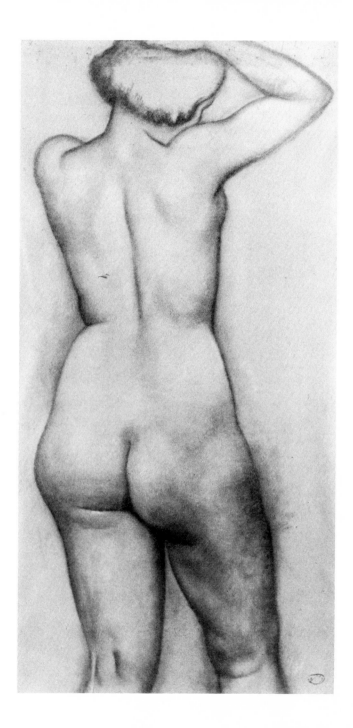

147

The American
(L'Américaine). 1935
Pastel on hand-made paper, 13¾ x 7⅞″
(35 x 20 cm.)
Not signed
Collection Dina Vierny, Paris

148

Three Pages of Sketches for the "Livret de
Folastries" by Ronsard
(Trois dessins projet illustrations pour le
"Livret de Folastries" de Ronsard). 1938
Pencil on tan paper, 12½ x 9½″ each
(32 x 24.1 cm.)
Not signed
Collection Dina Vierny, Paris

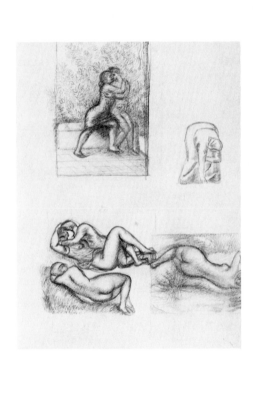

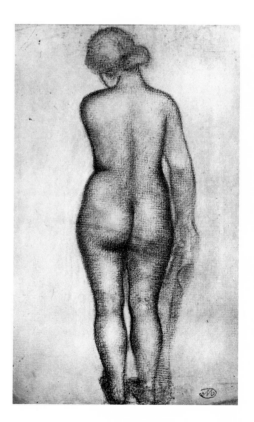

149
Back of Standing Girl
(Dos de jeune fille debout). 1939
Charcoal on antique laid paper, 14 x 9″
(35.5 x 23 cm.)
Signed l.r. with monogram
Collection Dina Vierny, Paris

150

Dina: Large Nude with a Braid
(Dina: Grand nu à la tresse). 1939

Charcoal and white chalk on gray wrapping
paper, 37⅜ x 52⅜″ (95 x 133 cm.)

Signed l.r. with monogram

Collection Dina Vierny, Paris

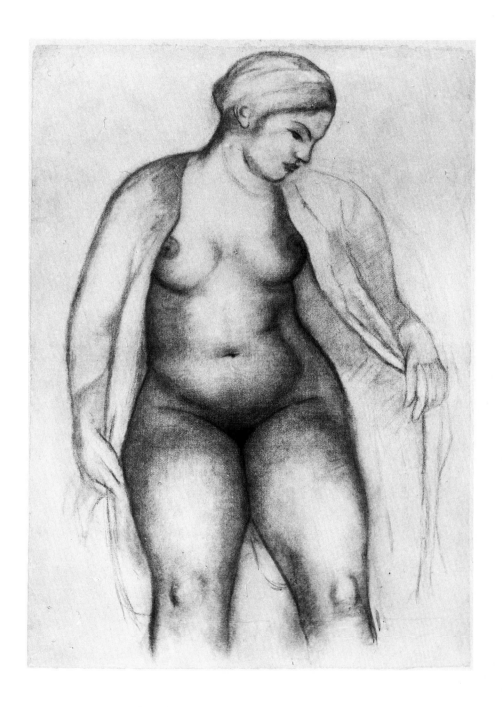

151

*Dina Seated, Facing Front
(Dina assise de face).* 1939

Charcoal on hand-made paper, 41⅜ x 30"
(105 x 76 cm.)

Not signed

Collection Dina Vierny, Paris

152

Dina: Study
(Dina: étude). 1939

Charcoal on hand-made paper, 26 x 41½″
(66 x 105.5 cm.)

Not signed

Collection Dina Vierny, Paris

153

*Portrait of Dina
(Portrait de Dina).* 1939

Pencil on antique laid paper, 12¼ x 8¼"
(31 x 22 cm.)

Signed l.r. with monogram

Collection Dina Vierny, Paris

154

*Back of a Swimmer
(Dos de nageuse).* 1940

Sanguine and white chalk on green wrapping
paper, 8¼ x 13" (21 x 33 cm.)

Signed l.r. with monogram

Collection Dina Vierny, Paris

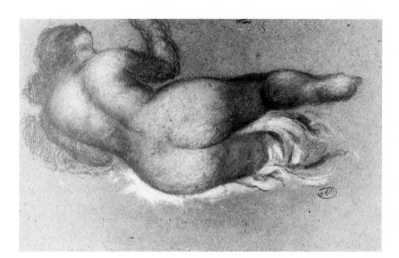

155

Dina. 1940

Sanguine and white chalk on gray wrapping paper,
11 x 14½″ (28 x 37 cm.)

Signed l.c. with monogram

Collection Dina Vierny, Paris

156

*Study for "Harmony," Facing Front
(Etude de face pour "L'Harmonie").* 1940

Charcoal and chalk on butcher's paper,
14⅛ x 8¼″ (36 x 21 cm.)

Not signed

Collection Dina Vierny, Paris

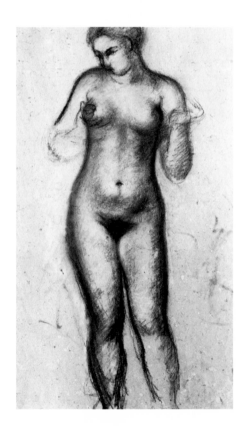

157

Dina with Hair
(Dina en cheveux). 1941

Charcoal on gray wrapping paper, 17¾ x 10⅝″
(45 x 27 cm.)

Signed l.r. with monogram

Collection Dina Vierny, Paris

158

Dina from the Back
(Dina de dos). 1941

Charcoal and chalk on butcher's paper, 9⅞ x 14⅛″
(25 x 36 cm.)

Signed l.r. with monogram

Collection Dina Vierny, Paris

159

Tulip

(Tulipe). 1941

Sanguine on hand-made paper, 11⅜ x 7⅞″
(29 x 20 cm.)

Signed l.r. with monogram; inscribed by the
artist "Tulipe"

Collection Dina Vierny, Paris

160

Dina, Full-Face and Profile

(Dina de face et de profil). 1941

Charcoal on gray wrapping paper, 9½ x 13¼″
(24 x 33.5 cm.)

Signed l.l. with monogram

Collection Dina Vierny, Paris

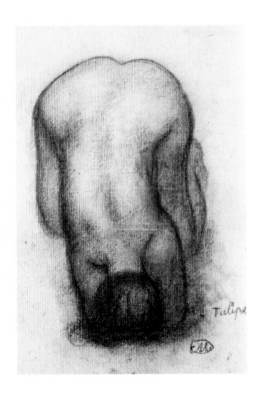

161

Woman with a Shirt
(Femme à la chemise). 1941

Sanguine and white chalk on gray wrapping
paper, 17¾ x 10¼" (45 x 26 cm.)

Signed l.l. with monogram

Collection Dina Vierny, Paris

162

Dina: Reclining with Drapery
(Dina: couchée à la draperie). 1942

Charcoal, pencil and chalk on butcher's paper,
8½ x 13¾" (21.5 x 35 cm.)

Signed l.r. with monogram

Collection Dina Vierny, Paris

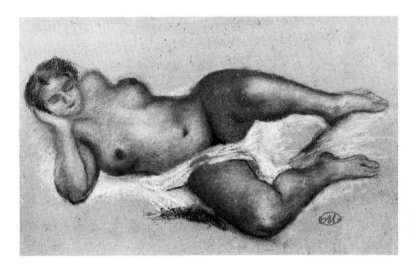

163

Dina: Profile for "Harmony"
(Dina: profil pour "L'Harmonie"). 1942

Charcoal on butcher's paper, 15⅜ x 10⅝"
(39 x 27 cm.)

Signed l.r. with monogram

Collection Dina Vierny, Paris

164

Back of Dina
(Dos de Dina). 1943

Sanguine and white chalk on gray wrapping
paper, 10⅝ x 14⅛" (27 x 36 cm.)

Signed l.r. with monogram

Collection Dina Vierny, Paris

165

Publius Vergilius Maro: Eclogae
Cranach Press, Weimar, 1925
43 woodcuts
Collection Dina Vierny, Paris

166

Emile Verhaeren, *Belle chair*
Editions d'Art Edouard Pelletan, Helleu et Sergent,
Paris, 1931
11 lithographs, 3 woodcuts
Collection Dina Vierny, Paris

167

Ovide, *L'Art d'aimer*
Philippe Gonin, Paris, 1935
15 woodcuts, 12 lithographs
Collection Dina Vierny, Paris

168

Longus, *Daphnis et Chloé*
Philippe Gonin, Paris, 1938
43 woodcuts
Collection Dina Vierny, Paris

169

Paul Verlaine, *Chansons pour elle*
Editions d'Art Pelletan, Hilleu et Sergent, Paris,
1939
28 woodcuts
Collection Dina Vierny, Paris

170

Pierre de Ronsard, *Le Livret de Folastries*
Ambroise Vollard, Paris, 1938
43 etchings
Collection Dina Vierny, Paris

171

9 letters to John Rewald, 1938-41

CHRONOLOGY

The dates in the following chronology are based primarily on information supplied by Dina Vierny.

1861

Born December 8 at Banyuls-sur-Mer, a fishing village on the Mediterranean near the Spanish border. Raised by his aunt and grandfather. Attends school at Banyuls, later in Peripignan, where his gift for drawing is recognized. He decides at an early age to become a painter.

1881

Despite extreme poverty, goes to Paris to study painting. Fails entrance examinations to *Ecole des Beaux-Arts* several times.

1885

Finally admitted to *Ecole des Beaux-Arts*, where he studies painting with Gérôme and Cabanel.

1889

Meets Bourdelle, with whom he forms close friendship.

1892

Deeply impressed by Gauguin's Brittany paintings. Meets Denis at about this time. Disgusted with *Ecole des Beaux-Arts*, he becomes interested in tapestry; studies Gothic tapestries at Musée de Cluny. Meets Gauguin who encourages him. Abandons painting for tapestry making.

1893

Establishes small tapestry workshop in aunt's house at Banyuls. Exhibits tapestry at *Salon de la Société Nationale*, Paris. He shows there regularly until the founding of the *Salon d'Automne* in 1904.

1893-95

Marries Clotilde Narcisse, a worker in his tapestry studio; they have a son, Lucien.

1894

Returns to Paris. Executes first woodcuts. Shows tapestry and embroidery at *La Libre esthétique*, Brussels. Continues to live in great poverty.

1895

First sculpture.

1896

Shows sculpture for first time at *Salon*, continues to produce tapestry. Associates with *Nabis* artists.

1898

Exhibits terra cottas at *La Libre esthétique*, Brussels.

1899

Moves to Villeneuve-Saint-Georges, near Paris.

1900

His house at Villeneuve-Saint-Georges is frequented by a circle of artists and writers, including Denis, Roussel, Thadée Natanson, Rippl-Ronai, Bonnard, Vuillard, Matisse, most of whom are *Nabis*. Forced by deteriorating eyesight to abandon tapestry, he turns exclusively to sculpture. Works in terra cotta, ceramic, varnished clay; gives up wood carving. Introduced by Vuillard to Vollard who buys some terra cottas, casts them in bronze. Financial situation begins to improve slightly.

1902

Participates in group exhibition at Berthe Weil's, Paris. First one-man exhibition at Galerie Ambroise Vollard, Paris, a critical success, praised by Octave Mirbeau and Rodin. Begins monumental *La Méditerranée*.

1903

Moves to Marly-le-Roy, near Paris, where he thereafter spends summers, but winters in Banyuls.

1904

Shows for first time at *Salon d'Automne*.

1905

La Méditerranée shown at *Salon*, admired by Gide, among others. Through Rodin meets Count Kessler, who becomes his friend and patron. Kessler commissions a relief, *Le Désir*, completed 1907, and purchases *La Méditerranée*.

Commissioned to execute memorial to revolutionary Louis-Auguste Blanqui, *L'Action enchaînée*. Intense friendship with Matisse.

1907

Makes portrait bust of Renoir. Renoir is inspired by Maillol to attempt sculpture.

1908

Trip to Greece with Kessler, who commissions woodcut illustrations of Virgil's *Eclogues*. These are not published until 1925.

1909

La Nuit shown at *Salon d'Automne*, where it is given the place of honor.

1910

Pomone shown at *Salon d'Automne*; international recognition and first notice by Parisian press follows. *Pomone* bought by Russian collector Morosoff, who commissions three more female figures, *L'Eté, Le Printemps, Flore*; the four together comprise *Les Saisons*.

1912-13

A group of Maillol's artist friends commission *Monument à Cézanne* from him. First studies for it executed.

1914-15

Accused of espionage because of association with Kessler, he is eventually exonerated.

1919-23

Executes war memorials for towns of Céret, Port-Vendres.

1925

First exhibition in United States, Albright Art Gallery, Buffalo. *Monument à Cézanne* rejected by town of Aix; it is bought but not erected by city of Paris.

1926

First exhibition in New York, Brummer Gallery.

1928

Trip to Germany.

1929

Monument à Cézanne installed in Tuileries Gardens, Paris.

1930

Begins war memorial for town of Banyuls. Commission for monument to Debussy, for which he makes preliminary studies. Starts work on what will be central figure of *Les Trois nymphes*. Trip to Germany, where he visits Kessler.

1933

Inauguration of monument to Debussy at Saint-Germain-en-Laye and of Banyuls memorial.

1936

Trip to Italy

1938

Begins work on commissions for monument to French aviators, *L'Air*, for city of Toulouse, and memorial to Henri Barbusse, *La Rivière*.

1941-42

Paints, does many drawings. Works on his last sculpture, *L'Harmonie*, posed for by Dina Vierny, his only model for the last ten years of his life.

1944

Injured in automobile accident, September 15. He dies at Banyuls, September 27.

SELECTED LIST OF EXHIBITIONS

One-man Exhibitions

Galerie Ambroise Vollard, Paris, 1902

Bernheim Jeune & Cie., Paris, January 23-February 1, 1911, *Les Tapisseries d'Aristide Maillol*. Checklist.

Galerie Flechtheim, Berlin, 1919. Catalogue text by Count Harry Kessler.

The Buffalo Fine Arts Academy, Albright Art Gallery, Buffalo, New York, November 15-December 14, 1925, *Exhibition of Sculpture and Drawings by Aristide Maillol 1925-26*. Catalogue texts by Augustus John and Anna Glenny Dunbar. Traveled to Brummer Gallery, New York, January 18-February 13, 1926, *Exhibition of Sculpture and Drawings by Aristide Maillol*. Checklist.

Memorial Art Gallery, Rochester, New York, April 1927, *Sculpture and Drawings by Aristide Maillol*. Catalogue.

Goupil Gallery, London, October 1928.

Galerie Flechtheim, Berlin, November 29-Christmas 1928, *Maillol*. Traveled to Galerie Giroux, Brussels, February 1929. Catalogue with text by Count Harry Kessler. Translated into English by J. H. Mason as *Maillol*, London, 1930.

Brummer Gallery, New York, January 3-February 28, 1933, *Sculpture by Maillol*. Pamphlet text by Conger Goodyear.

Kunsthalle Basel, August 5-September 16, 1933, *Aristide Maillol*. Catalogue texts by Ernst Suter and Otto Roos.

Valentine Gallery, New York, January 3-29, 1938, *"Venus:" A Bronze by Maillol*. Checklist includes *Georges Rouault and XXth Century French Masters*.

Buchholz Gallery, New York, January 31-February 24, 1940, *Exhibition Aristide Maillol*. Catalogue with text by John Rewald, reprinted from *Maillol*, New York, 1939.

The Arts Club of Chicago, December 4-28, 1940, *Aristide Maillol*. Checklist.

Galerie Louis Carré, Paris, December 15-31, 1941, *Maillol: dessins et pastels*. Pamphlet text by Maurice Denis.

Weyhe Gallery, New York, January 5-31, 1942, *Aristide Maillol: Drawings, Prints, Sculpture, Photographs*. Announcement.

Kunsthalle Basel, November 25-December 31, 1944, *Gedächtnis-Schau Aristide Maillol*. Catalogue.

The Buffalo Fine Arts Academy, Albright Art Gallery, New York, April 14-May 23, 1945, *Aristide Maillol*. Catalogue text by Andrew C. Ritchie, selections from interview with Maillol by Judith Cladel, translated from *Aristide Maillol: sa vie—son oeuvre—ses idées*, Paris, 1937.

Buchholz Gallery, New York, June 6-30, 1945, *Aristide Maillol 1861-1944*. Checklist.

Blanch's Konstgalleri, Stockholm, September-October 1947, *Aristide Maillol 1861-1944: Gobelänger, Skulpturer, Oljemalningar, Pasteller och Teckningar*. Catalogue text by Gustaf Engwall.

Kunsthaus Zurich, September 6-mid-November 1947, *Maillol: Gemälde und Werkzeichnungen*.

Galerie Charpentier, Paris, 1947, *Exposition Maillol*. Catalogue texts by Jules Romains and Waldemar George.

Galerie Dina Vierny, Paris, 1947, *Hommage à Maillol*.

Petit Palais, Paris, May 1947, *Aristide Maillol*. Catalogue. Traveled to Ny Carlsberg Glyptotek, Copenhagen, 1947. Catalogue with text by Haavard Rostrup.

Galerie Karin Hielscher, Munich, November 1950-January 1951, *Aristide Maillol*. Catalogue text by John Rewald.

Buchholz Gallery, Curt Valentin, New York, February 6-March 3, 1951, *Aristide Maillol: 1861-1944*. Catalogue includes selections from interview with Maillol by Judith Cladel translated from *Aristide Maillol: sa vie—son oeuvre—ses idées*, Paris, 1937.

Kunstverein, Dusseldorf, 1951.

Galerie Blanche, Stockholm, March-April 1954, *Aristide Maillol: Skulpturer, Teckningar, Grafik*. Catalogue text by G. E.

Gimpel Gallery, London, 1955.

Musée Cantini, Marseille, July-August 1956, *Aristide Maillol*. Catalogue text by Jean Cassou.

Paul Rosenberg & Co., New York, March 3-29, 1958, *An Exhibition of Original Pieces of Sculpture by Aristide Maillol 1861-1944*. Catalogue texts by John Rewald and Dina Vierny. Traveled to: Philadelphia Museum of Art, April 15-May 15; The Cleveland Museum of Art, July-August; The Toledo Museum of Art, September 15-October 15; Museum of Fine Arts, Boston, November 15-December 15; Albright Art Gallery, Buffalo, January 15-February 15, 1959; The Minneapolis Art Institute, March 1-April 5; City Art Museum of St. Louis, April 24-May 24; California Palace of the Legion of Honor, San Francisco, September 10-October 10; Los Angeles County Museum, November 3-December 20; Dallas Museum of Fine Arts, January 17-February 14, 1960.

Galerie Daber, Paris, April 20-May 20, 1961, *Maillol: Exposition—Hommage du centenaire de sa naissance 1861-1961*. Catalogue texts by Alfred Daber and Henri Frère.

Musée National d'Art Moderne, Paris, June 23-October 2, 1961, *Hommage à Aristide Maillol (1861-1944)*. Catalogue text by Jean Cassou.

Kunstverein in Hamburg, October 27, 1961-January 7, 1962, *Aristide Maillol*. Catalogue text by Alfred Hentzen. Traveled to: Stedelijk Museum, Amsterdam, February 16-March 19 (catalogue); Frankfurter Kunstverein, March 27-May 6; Württembergischer Kunstverein, Stuttgart, May 19-July 8; Haus der Kunst, Munich, July 21-October 7 (catalogue with texts by Alfred Hentzen and Dina Vierny).

[National Museum of Western Art], Tokyo, August 2-September 15, 1963, *Maillol*. Catalogue text in Japanese.

Galerie Pierre, Stockholm, 1963. Traveled to Galerie Artek, Helsinki, 1963.

Musée des Beaux-Arts, Neuchâtel, 1964.

Galerie Pierre, Stockholm, 1967.

Perls Galleries, New York, March 18-April 18, 1970, *Aristide Maillol (1861-1944)*. Catalogue text by John Rewald.

Palais de la Méditerranée, Nice, 1970.

Gimpel Fils, London, October 26-November 20, 1971, *Maillol*. Catalogue.

Palais des Arts, Brest, 1971.

Galerie Conkright, Caracas, 1973.

[Prefectural Museum of Modern Art], Hyogo, Kobe, October 10-November 10, 1974, *Maillol*. Catalogue text in Japanese. Traveled to: [Prefectural Museum of Art], Hiroshima, November 30-December 22; [Prefectural Museum of Art], Ehime, Matsuyama, January 5-19, 1975; Museum of the City of Kitakyushu, January 25-February 23; MRO Hall, Kanazawa, March 10-April 3; Mitsukoshi Gallery, Tokyo, April 15-20.

Centre Artistique et Littéraire de Rochechouart, March 30-June 3, 1974. Catalogue texts by Michel Hoog and John Rewald.

Gimpel Fils, London, March 11-April 12, 1975, *Aristide Maillol: 1861-1944*. Pamphlet with checklist.

Group Exhibitions

Salon de la Société Nationale, Paris, 1893-1903.

Salon d'Automne, Paris, 1904, 1905, 1907, 1909, 1910, 1921, 1922, 1926, 1928.

Salon de La Libre esthétique, Brussels, 1894, 1898.

Galerie Berthe Weil, Paris, 1902.

Leicester Galleries, London, November-December 1919, *Pictures by Henri Matisse and Sculpture by Maillol*. Catalogue.

Cleveland Museum of Art, Fall 1926. *Fifty Years of French Art; Sculpture and Drawings by Maillol*.

Worcester Art Museum, Worcester, Massachusetts, March 13-27, 1927, *Exhibition of Sculpture, Drawings and Lithographs by Aristide Maillol and other French Artists*. Catalogue text by G. W. E.

Phillips Memorial Gallery, Washington, D.C., December 1927-January 1928, *Leaders of French Art Today*. Catalogue text by Duncan Phillips.

Wildenstein Galleries, New York, January 11-February 1, 1928, *Exhibition of Modern European Sculpture*. Catalogue text by Anna Glenny Dunbar. Traveled in United States.

The Museum of Modern Art, New York, March 13-April 2, 1930, *Wilhelm Lehmbruck; Aristide Maillol*. Catalogue text by Jere Abbot.

The Museum of Modern Art, New York, April 27-September 2, 1936, *Modern Painters and Sculptors as Illustrators*. Catalogue text by Monroe Wheeler.

Petit Palais, Paris, *Les Maîtres de l'art indépendant 1895-1937*, June-October 1937. Catalogue texts by Raymond Escholier and Albert Sarraut.

Buchholz Gallery, New York, December 4-30, 1937, *Aristide Maillol: Drawings, Lithographs, Etchings, Woodcuts; Renée Sintenis: Sculpture, Etchings, Woodcuts*. Checklist.

Stedelijk Museum, Amsterdam, July-September 1939, *Rondom Rodin*. Catalogue.

The Institute of Modern Art, Boston, January 31-February 26, 1939, *Show of Sculpture: Charles Despiau, Aristide Maillol*. Catalogue texts by Frank Crowninshield (Despiau) and Joseph A. Coletti (Maillol).

The Museum of Modern Art, New York, May 10-September 30, 1939, *Art in Our Time*. Catalogue.

The Museum of Modern Art, New York, [1939], *Six Modern Sculptors: Barlach, Despiau, Epstein, Kolbe, Lachaise, Maillol*. Pamphlet.

Cincinnati Art Museum, November 2-27, 1940, *Three Modern Sculptors: Gaston Lachaise, Georg Kolbe, Aristide Maillol*. Organized by The Cincinnati Art Society. Pamphlet.

Buchholz Gallery, New York, November 18-December 6, 1941, *Wilhelm Lehmbruck; Aristide Maillol*. Catalogue text by Jere Abbot, reprinted from *Wilhelm Lehmbruck; Aristide Maillol*, The Museum of Modern Art, New York, 1930.

Buchholz Gallery, New York, November 10-December 5, 1942. Checklist.

Buchholz Gallery, New York, December 8-26, 1942, *Seventy-Five Selected Prints; Small Sculpture by Maillol; Casts in Stone by John B. Flannagan*. Checklist.

Fogg Museum of Art, Cambridge, Massachusetts, May 4-29, 1943, *Masters of Four Arts: Wright, Maillol, Picasso, Stravinsky*. Catalogue.

Redfern Gallery, London, October 7-30, 1943, *Robin Darwin; A. Maillol; Roger Descombes*. Checklist.

The Museum of Modern Art, New York, February 16-May 10, 1944, *Modern Drawings*. Catalogue text by Monroe Wheeler.

Musée de Lyon, June 9-July 1, 1945, *4 retrospectives: Maillol, Vuillard, Boussingault, La Patellière*. Catalogue text by Claude Roger-Marx.

Ny Carlsberg Glyptotek, Copenhagen, July-October 1945, *Fransk Kunst: Maleri og Skulptur fra det 19. og 20. Aarhundrede*. Catalogue text by Haavard Rostrup.

Gemeentemuseum, The Hague, June 30-September 4, 1950, *Rodin, Bourdelle, Maillol, Despiau*. Catalogue.

Museum of Fine Arts, Boston, May 4-July 16, 1961, *The Artist and the Book 1860-1960*. Catalogue notes by Philip Hofer.

Musée des Augustins, Toulouse, 1961, *Achille Laugé et ses amis Bourdelle et Maillol*. Catalogue texts by Paul Mesple, Albert Sarraut and Charles Pornon.

Palais de la Méditerranée, Nice, December 1962-January 1963, *Sculpture Méditerranéenne*. Catalogue text by C. Goldscheider.

The Baltimore Museum of Art, December 2, 1969-February 1, 1970, *The Partial Figure in Modern Sculpture*. Catalogue text by Albert E. Elsen.

Hayward Gallery, London, June 20-September 23, 1973, *Pioneers of Modern Sculpture*. Catalogue text by Albert E. Elsen.

SELECTED BIBLIOGRAPHY

Monographs and Special Magazine Issues

Octave Mirbeau, *Aristide Maillol*, Paris, 1921.

Maurice Denis, *A. Maillol*, Paris, 1925.

Alfred Kuhn, *Aristide Maillol: Landschaft, Werke, Gespräche*, Leipzig, 1925.

Marc Lafargue, *Aristide Maillol: sculpture et lithographe*, Paris, 1925.

Pierre Camo, *Aristide Maillol*, Paris, 1926.

Marc Lafargue, *Grande ode au jardin de Marly et à Aristide Maillol*, Paris, 1928.

René-Jean, *Maillol*, Paris, 1934.

Judith Cladel, *Aristide Maillol: sa vie—son oeuvre—ses ideés*, Paris, 1937.

Marie Dormoy, *Arts et métiers graphiques*, Paris, 1937. Maillol issue.

Paul Sentenac, *Aristide Maillol*, Paris, 1937.

John Rewald, "Les ateliers de Maillol," *Le Point*, troisième année, XVII, November 1938, pp. 201-240. Maillol issue.

Heinrich Appel, *Das Meisterwerk Maillol*, Basel, [1939].

John Rewald, *Maillol*, London, Paris, New York, 1939.

Maurice Denis, Pierre du Colombier, *Maillol: dessins et pastels*, Paris, 1942.

Julio E. Payró, *Aristide Maillol*, Buenos Aires, 1942.

John Rewald, *The Woodcuts of Aristide Maillol: A Complete Catalogue*, New York, 1943.

Paul Valéry, Maurice Denis, Auguste Perret, Pierre du Colombier, Claude Roy, Jean Lods, *Maillol*, Paris, 1943.

Marquette Bouvier, *Aristide Maillol*, Lausanne, 1945.

Marc Lafargue, Octave Mirbeau, Pierre Camo, Jean Girou, *Aspects de Maillol*, Albi, 1945.

Pierre Camo, André Susplugas, Henri Frère, Joseph-Sébastien Pons, Ludovic Massé, *Cahier des amis de l'art*, no. 10, 1946. Maillol issue.

Jean Charbonneaux, *Maillol*, Paris, 1947.

Claude Roy, *Maillol vivant*, Geneva, 1947.

Jules Romains, *Les Maîtres du dessin: Maillol*, Paris, 1948.

Pierre Camo, *Maillol mon ami: sa vie, son amité, son art*, Lausanne, 1950.

John Rewald, *Aristide Maillol 1861-1944*, Paris, 1950.

Boris Ternovetz, *Aristide Maillol*, Milan, 1950.

Henri Frère, *Conversations de Maillol*, Geneva, 1956.

Rolf Linnekamp, *Aristide Maillol und der goldene Schnitt der Fläche: Ein neues Gesetz der Geometrie*, Hamburg, 1957.

Hermann Uhde-Bernays, *Aristide Maillol*, Dresden, 1957.

Berthold Hackelsberger, *Aristide Maillol: La Méditerranée*, Stuttgart, 1960.

Rolf Linnekamp, *Aristide Maillol: Die grossen Plastiken*, Munich, 1960.

Jiri Masin, *Aristide Maillol*, Prague, 1960.

H. R. Hoetink, *Aristide Maillol: "La Méditerranée,"* 1963.

Waldemar George, *Aristide Maillol et l'âme de la sculpture*, Neuchâtel, 1964? Translated by Diana Imber as *Aristide Maillol*, Greenwich, Connecticut, 1965?

Marcel Guérin, *Catalogue raisonné de l'oeuvre gravé et lithographié de Aristide Maillol*, 2 vols., Geneva, 1965, 1967.

Denys Chevalier, *Maillol*, Paris, 1970.

Waldemar George, *Maillol*, Paris, 1971.

General Books

Julius Meier-Graefe, *Entwickelungsgeschichte der modernen Kunst: vergleichende Betrachtung der bildenden Künste, als Beitrag zu einer neuen Asthetik*, 3 vols., Stuttgart, 1904, vol. I, pp. 395-400; vol. III, pp. 190-191; Translated by Florence Simmonds and George W. Chrystal as *Modern Art: Being a Contribution to a New System of Aesthetics*, 5 vols., London, 1908, vol. II, pp. 75-79.

Jozsef Rippl-Ronaï, *Emlékezései*, Budapest, 1911.

Lorado Taft, *Modern Tendencies in Sculpture*, Chicago, 1917, pp. 38, 40, 65.

Félix Fénéon, *L'Art moderne et quelques aspects de l'art autrefois*, 2 vols., Paris, 1919.

Maurice Denis, *Théories 1890-1910 du symbolisme et de Gauguin vers un nouvel ordre classique*, Paris, 1920, pp. 235-244.

Alfred Kuhn, *Die Neuere Plastik von 1800 bis zur Gegenwart*, Munich, 1922, pp. 73, 87, 90-94, 100-101, 105, 110, 113, 116, 128.

Léon Werth, *Quelques peintres*, Paris, 1923, pp. 203-211.

Adolphe Basler, *La Sculpture moderne en France*, Paris, 1928, pp. 40-46.

Stanley Casson, *Some Modern Sculptors*, New York, 1928, pp. 30-59.

Rainer-Maria Rilke, *Briefe aus den Jahren 1906 bis 1907*, Leipzig, 1930.

William Rothenstein, *Men and Memories*, vol. II, 1900-22, New York, 1932, pp. 86, 87, 195, 198-200.

R. H. Wilenski, *The Meaning of Modern Sculpture*, London, 1932, pp. 121-123.

Paul Fierens, *Sculpteurs d'aujourd'hui*, Paris, 1933, pp. 9-10+.

Ambroise Vollard, *Recollections of a Picture Dealer*, Boston, 1936, pp. 24, 92, 146, 197, 204, 206, 207, 249, 261, 305. Translated from original French manuscript by Violet M. Macdonald.

Carola Giedion-Welcker, *Moderne Plastik*, Zurich, 1937, pp. 7, 30, 96. Revised and expanded as *Contemporary Sculpture: An Evolution in Volume and Space*, New York, 1960, pp. x, xi, xxvii, 26, 27, 34, 52, 339, 341.

Claude Roger-Marx, *French Original Engravings from Manet to the Present Time*, London, Paris, New York, 1939, pp. 47-48.

Claude Roger-Marx, *Anthologie du livre illustré par les peintres et sculpteurs de l'Ecole de Paris*, Geneva, 1946, pp. 62-64.

Jacques Baschet, *Sculpteurs de ce temps*, Paris, 1946, pp. 7-23.

Graham Reynolds, *Twentieth Century Drawings*, London, 1946, pp. 32, 33.

W. R. Valentiner, *Origins of Modern Sculpture*, New York, 1946, pp. 4, 13, 29, 30, 61, 101, 131.

Georg Kolbe, *Auf Wegen der Kunst*, Berlin, 1949, pp. 23-24.

Andrew Carnduff Ritchie, *Sculpture of the Twentieth Century*, New York, 1952, pp. 18-21, 39, 72-82, 229, 236.

Jean Selz, *Modern Sculpture: Origins and Evolution*, New York, 1963. Translated from the French by Annette Michelson, pp. 151-157.

George Heard Hamilton, *Painting and Sculpture in Europe, 1880 to 1940*, Baltimore, 1967, pp. 95-98.

A. M. Hammacher, *The Evolution of Modern Sculpture: Tradition and Innovation* New York, 1969 ?, pp. 50, 64, 66, 68, 80, 82-83, 107, 108, 124, 146, 151, 173, 196, 204, 256, 259.

Werner Hofmann, "Uber Matisse, Maillol und Brancusi," *Museum und Kunst: Beiträge für Alfred Hentzen*, Hamburg, 1970, pp. 97-108.

Albert E. Elsen, *Origins of Modern Sculpture: Pioneers and Premises*, New York, 1974, pp. viii-ix, 12-16, 23, 29-30, 31, 32, 46, 67-68, 71, 74, 76, 84-85, 90, 97, 103, 110, 116, 119-123, 130, 138-140, 153, 154, 156-157. Enlarged and revised version of Hayward Gallery, London, 1973, catalogue text (see group exhibitions list).

Periodicals

Félicien Fagus, "Durio, Bocquet, Maillol," *La Revue blanche*, January 1, 1902.

Félicien Fagus, "Maillol," *La Revue blanche*, August 1, 1902.

Octave Mirbeau, "Aristide Maillol," *La Revue*, series 4, vol. 55, April 1905, pp. 321-344.

Charles Morice, "Le Salon d'Automne," *Mercure de France*, December 1, 1905.

Maurice Denis, "Aristide Maillol," *L'Occident*, vol. 8, 1905, pp. 241-249.

André Gide, "Promenade au Salon d'Automne," *Gazette des Beaux-Arts*, vol. 34, no. 3, 1905, pp. 475-485.

Maurice Denis, "Aristide Maillol," *Kunst und Künstler*, Jahr. 4, 1906, pp. 519-522.

Emile Bernard, "Réflexions à propos du Salon d'Automne," *La Rénovation esthetique*, December 1907.

Maurice Denis, "Aristide Maillol," *L'Art et les artistes*, vol. VIII, January 1909, pp. 156-160.

Roger Fry, "The Sculptures of Maillol," *The Burlington Magazine*, vol. 17, no. 85, April 1910, pp. 26-32.

Léon Werth, "Aristide Maillol," *Kunst für Alle*, vol. XXVI, no. 12, March 15, 1911, pp. 276-283.

Claude Roger-Marx, "La Gravure de sculpteurs en France," *Byblis*, 1913.

Paul Sentenac, "Variétés: Un Livre d'art décoré par Aristide Maillol," *L'Art et les artistes*, June 1914, pp. 184-186.

Sheldon Cheney, "Maillol, Giant of Sculpture," *International Studio*, vol. LXXVIII, no. 317, October 1923, pp. 3-11.

Waldemar George, "Les Terres-cuites de Maillol," *L'Amour de l'art*, année 4, 1923, pp. 695-700.

Waldemar George, "Aristide Maillol," *The Arts*, vol. 5, no. 2, February 1924, pp. 84-109.

André Levinson, "Sculpteurs de ce temps," *L'Amour de l'art*, November 1924, pp. 377-391.

Arnold Ronnebeck, "The Teachings of Maillol (From a Paris Diary)," *The Arts*, vol. 8, no. 1, July 1925, pp. 38-40.

"Maillol Speaks," *The Arts*, vol. 8, no. 1, July 1925, pp. 35-37.

Christian Zervos, "Aristide Maillol," *L'Art d'aujourd'hui*, année 2, no. 4, Autumn 1925, pp. 33-48. Includes "Hommages à Maillol," series of statements about Maillol.

Albert Dreyfus, "Ein Besuch bei Aristide Maillol," *Kunst und Künstler*, Jahr. 25, 1926, pp. 83-86.

Paul Clemen, "Aristide Maillol und die französische Plastik von Heute," *Die Kunst für Alle*, Jahr. 42, 1926-27, pp. 41-54.

Jean Alazard, "Aristide Maillol," *Dedalo*, vol. 1, no. 3, August 1927, pp. 178-198.

Louise Gebhard Cann, "The Engraved Work of Maillol," *The Arts*, vol. 14, no. 4, October 1928, pp. 200-203.

Count Harry Kessler, "Warum Maillol Vergils Eklogen illustriert hat," *Der Querschnitt*, November 1928.

Karl Scheffler, "Aristide Maillol," *Kunst und Künstler*, Jahr. 28, January 1929.

Jules Romains, "Maillol," *Formes*, no. 4, April 1930, pp. 5-7.

André Fontainas, "L'Oeuvre récente d'Aristide Maillol/Aristide Maillol's Recent Work," *Formes*, no. 19, November 1931, pp. 148-150.

Paul Sentenac, "Autour des oeuvres récentes d'Aristide Maillol," *L'Art et les artistes*, no. 21, March 1931, pp. 192-198.

René-Jean, "Aristide Maillol à Marly," *Beaux-Arts*, no. 39, September 29, 1933.

Waldemar George, "Le Sentiment antique dans l'art moderne," *L'Amour de l'art*, no. 2, February 1935, pp. 51-56.

Alfred Hentzen, "Buch-Illustrationen von Aristide Maillol," *Philobiblon Die Zeitschrift der Bücher-freunde*, Jahr. 10, no. 7, 1938, pp. 336-350.

John Rewald, "Aristide Maillol," *Marianne*, January 5, 1938.

John Rewald, "Les bois gravés d'Aristide Maillol," *Marianne*, September 14, 1938.

John Rewald, "Une nouvelle oeuvre de Maillol: 'L'Air,'" *Beaux-Arts*, no. 318, February 3, 1939, pp. 1, 4.

John Rewald, "Reflexions autour de la 'Pomone' d'Aristide Maillol," *La Renaissance*, no. 1, March 1939, pp. 9-16.

John Rewald, "For Aristide Maillol on his Eightieth Birthday, *Art News*, vol. XL, no. 16, December 1-14, 1941, pp. 19+.

Jean Giono, "Sur un très grand livre: 'Les Géorgiques' de Virgile, illustré par le sculpteur Maillol et imprimé par Phillipe Gonin," *Minotaure*, année 6, série 3, no. 12-13, May 1939, n.p. Reprinted in *Formes et Couleurs*, no. 2, 1942, pp. 43-50.

Hugo Weber, "Erinnerungen an Aristide Maillol," *Werk*, Jahr. 31, no. 12, December 1944, pp. 365-370.

Nicolas Rauch, "Peint et sculpteurs français dans l'art du livre moderne," *Formes et Couleurs*, no. 6, 1944, n.p.

Erwin Gradmann, "Maillol als Zeichner/Maillol as a Draughtsman," *Graphis*, Jahr. I, no. 7/8, April-June 1945, pp. 107-113.

Andrew C. Ritchie, "Maillol and the Eternal Feminine," *Art News*, vol. 44, no. 6, May 1-14, 1945, pp. 12-13.

John Rewald, "Last Visit with Maillol," *Magazine of Art*, vol. 38, no. 5, May 1945, pp. 164-167.

John Rewald, "Maillol illustrateur," *Le Portique*, no. 1, 1945, pp. 26-38.

Adam Fischer, "Aristide Maillol 1869-1944," *Kunsten Idag*, no. 3, Summer 1947, pp. 20-39.

Curt Schweicher, "Rodin und Maillol," *Werk*, Jahr. 34, no. 10, October 1947, pp. 329-36. Precis in French.

Hermann Uhde-Bernays, "Aristide Maillol," *Aussaat*, Jahr. 1, no. 12, 1947, pp. 22-25.

Thadée Natanson, "Souvenirs de Maillol," *Carrefour*, 1947.

Werner Gramberg, "Bemerkungen zur Entstehungsgeschichte der 'Rivière' von Aristide Maillol," *Jahrbuch der Hamburger Kunstsammlungen*, vol. 4, 1959, pp. 73-86.

Manfred Meinz, "Mediterrane Meditaties," *Bulletin Museum Boymans-van Beuningen*, vol. XIV, no. 2, 1963.

Patrick McCaughey, "The Monolith and Modernist Sculpture," *Art International*, vol. XIV, no. 9, November 1970, pp. 19-24.

Books illustrated by the artist

Publius Vergilius Maro, *Eclogae*, Cranach Press, Weimar, 1925, Latin and German text translated by Rudolf Alexander Schröder; 1926, Latin and French text translated by Marc Lafargue; 1927, Latin and English text translated by J. H. Mason. 43 woodcuts.

Les Quatre graveurs du mans. Editions de la Douce France, Paris, 1922. 1 woodcut.

Pierre Louyes, *Poésies*, Editions Crès & Cie, Paris, 1926. 1 lithograph.

Marc Lafargue, *Les Plaisirs et les regrets*, Garnier, Paris, 1928. 1 lithograph.

Emile Verhaeren, *Belle Chair*, Editions d'Art Edouard Pelletan, Helleu et Sergent, Paris, 1931. 11 lithographs, 3 woodcuts.

Ovide, *L'Art d'aimer*, Philippe Gonin, Paris, 1935, translated by Henry Borneque. 15 woodcuts, 12 lithographs.

Joseph S. Pons, *Cantilena*, Barcelona, 1937. 1 lithograph.

Longus, *Daphnis and Chloe*, A. Zwemmer, London, 1937, translated by George Thornley; *Daphnis et Chloé*, Philippe Gonin, Paris, 1938, translated by Amyot, revised and completed by P. L. Courier. 43 woodcuts.

The Verona Press Rhyme Sheets, No. 2: Verses from the Greek, The Oxford University Press, London, c. 1938. 1 woodcut.

Pierre de Ronsard, *Livret de Folastries*, Ambroise Vollard, Paris, 1938. 43 etchings.

Serge Lifar, *Pensées sur la danse*, Bordas, Paris, 1946. 7 reproductions of drawings.

J. S. Pons, *Concert d'été*, Flammarion, Paris, 1946. Woodcuts.

Paul Verlaine, *Chansons pour elle*, Editions d'Art Pelletan, Helleu et Sergent, Paris, 1939. 28 woodcuts.

Publius Vergilius Maro, *Georgica*, Philippe Gonin, Paris, 1943. 121 woodcuts.

Lucien, *Dialogue des courtisanes*, Paris, 1950. Posthumous lithographs.

Q. Horatius Flaccus, *Odes*, Philippe Gonin, Paris, 1958. Woodcuts.

PHOTOGRAPHIC CREDITS

Victor Amato, Washington, D.C.: Cat. no. 22

Urusla Bagel: Cat. nos. 127, 148

Oliver Baker, New York: Cat. no. 24

Photo Bulloz: Cat. nos. 12, 13

Robert David: Cat. nos. 7, 120-122, 125, 130-132, 136, 137, 139, 145, 156, 158, 159, 162

Courtesy Dominion Gallery, Montreal: Cat. nos. 19, 50

Courtesy Paul Drey Gallery, New York: Cat. nos. 35, 71

Courtesy The Fine Arts Museums of San Francisco: Cat. no. 82

Courtesy Fogg Art Museum, Harvard University, Cambridge, Massachusetts: Cat. no. 61

Courtesy The Alex Hillman Family Foundation: Cat. nos. 32, 33

Thomas d'Hoste, Paris: Cat. no. 6

Pierre Jamet, Paris: Cat. no. 68

Courtesy Mr. and Mrs. David Lloyd Kreeger: Cat. no. 63

Delmar Lipp, Washington, D.C.: Cat. no. 42

Robert E. Mates and Mary Donlon, New York: Cat. nos. 14, 25-29, 37, 39, 44, 47, 49, 59, 67, 70, 78, 80, 81, 87, 88, 92, 99, 105

Studio Maywald, Paris: Cat. nos. 3-5, 8, 10, 11, 15-18, 36, 48, 55-57, 60, 73, 74, 76, 77, 86, 93-95, 103, 107, 110, 112-119, 123, 124, 126, 128, 129, 133-135, 138, 140-144, 146, 147, 149-155, 157, 160, 161, 163, 164

Courtesy The Metropolitan Museum of Art, New York: Cat. nos. 43, 69, 101

Courtesy The Minneapolis Institute of Arts: Cat. no. 97

Courtesy The Museum of Modern Art, New York: Cat. nos. 46, 51, 65, 106

Courtesy National Gallery of Art, Washington, D.C.: Cat. no. 72

O. E. Nelson, New York: Cat. no. 62

Courtesy Perls Galleries, New York: Cat. nos. 23, 84, 89, 90, 102, 111

Eric Pollitzer, Hempstead, New York: Cat. no. 100

Courtesy San Francisco Museum of Art: Cat. no. 41

Sherwin Greenberg McCranahan & May Inc., Buffalo: Cat. no. 30

Courtesy Mr. and Mrs. Nathan Smooke: Cat. no. 66

Taylor and Dull, Inc., New York: Cat. nos. 34, 38, 40, 54, 58, 79, 104

Courtesy The University of Michigan Museum of Art: Cat. no. 21

Courtesy Dina Vierny, Paris: Cat. nos. 1, 9, 20, 52, 109

Courtesy Wildenstein & Company, New York: Cat. nos. 64, 83

All figures in the text and supplementary illustrations: John Rewald

EXHIBITION 75/6

4000 copies of this catalogue
designed by Malcolm Grear Designers,
typeset by Dumar Typesetting, Inc.,
have been printed by Foremost Lithograph Company
in December 1975 for the Trustees of
The Solomon R. Guggenheim Foundation